Faith and the Emotions

NATURAL POWERS	
Spiritual	**Cognitive:** *mind (intellect and reason)* **Appetitive:** *will*
Sensitive	**External cognitive:** *sight, hearing, smell, taste, touch* **Internal cognitive:** *common sense, imagination, memory, sensitive usefulness judgment* **Appetitive:** Emotions of the pleasure appetite: *love and hate, desire and aversion, joy and sadness* Emotions of the utility appetite: *Hope or ambition and courage, despair and fear, anger*

Natural powers, habits, and acts

	HABITS		ACTS
Innate	Synderesis (pre-conscience inclining to do good and avoid evil) Various innate predispositions	**Natural**	Conscience (act of the practical reason)
Acquired through natural effort	Intellectual and manual (physical) abilities Worked-out moral virtues Cultivated moral vices	**Worked out**	Formed conscience Consciously elicited good and evil acts
Infused by grace but subject to conscious development and growth	Theological virtues: *faith, hope, and charity* Gifts of the Holy Spirit: *wisdom, understanding, counsel, fortitude, knowledge, piety, fear of the Lord* Cardinal moral virtues: *prudence (creative resourcefulness), justice, fortitude, temperance* Numerous other moral virtues: *magnanimity, chastity, patience,* etc.	**Flowing from grace**	Conscience attentive to the suggestions of the Holy Spirit Acts of the theological and moral virtues Fruits of the Holy Spirit (Gal. 5:22–23) Beatitudes (Matt. 5:3–12)

Wojciech Giertych, O.P.
Theologian of the Papal Household

FAITH and the EMOTIONS

EWTN Publishing, Inc.
Irondale, Alabama

Original edition: *Wiara a Uczucia* (Wydanie pierwsze, 2019)
Copyright © 2025 by Wojciech Giertych, O.P.
English edition Copyright © 2025 by Wojciech Giertych, O.P.

Translated by **Weronika P. Cichosz**

Cover design by **Wojciech Giertych/Beata Początek**

Interior design by **Beata Początek**

Printed in the United States of America. All rights reserved.

Excerpts from the English translation of the *Catechism of the Catholic Church* for use in the United States of America copyright © 1994, United States Catholic Conference, Inc. — Libreria Editrice Vaticana. English translation of the *Catechism of the Catholic Church: Modifications from the Editio Typica* copyright © 1997, United States Conference of Catholic Bishops — Libreria Editrice Vaticana.

No part of this book may be reproduced, stored in a retrieval system, or transmitted in any form, or by any means, electronic, mechanical, photocopying, or otherwise, without the prior written permission of the publisher, except by a reviewer, who may quote brief passages in a review.

EWTN Publishing, Inc.
5817 Old Leeds Road, Irondale, AL 35210
Distributed by Sophia Institute Press, Box 5284, Manchester, NH 03108.

Paperback ISBN 978-1-68278-423-5
Ebook ISBN 978-1-68278-424-2

Library of Congress Control Number: 2025941446

First printing

CONTENTS

Preface to the English Edition ix

Preface xi

I. What Are the Emotions? 1

II. The Place of the Emotions in the Psyche 6

III. Faith Opening Up to Grace 13

IV. Faith Is Followed Up with Hope and Charity 19

V. Emotional Difficulties 24

VI. Attempts at Dealing with the Emotions 30

VII. Grace Within the Emotions 34

VIII. Emotions Directed by the Will 40

IX. Blocked Emotions 46

X. Fear Neurosis 52

XI. Energy Neurosis 59

XII. Why Is This So Difficult? 65

XIII. Sexual Emotions 73

XIV. Assertive Emotions 80

XV. Happiness 86

XVI. Atonement 92

XVII. Afterword 98

Further Reading 103

Citations 104

Image Credits 108

About the Author 109

Preface to the English Edition

In this book, I attempt to present, in a simplified way, the basic teachings of moral theology concerning the emotions. I have published in Polish two similar books on "Faith and Freedom" and "Faith and Responsibility," but I have not yet had them translated into English. Together, they cover a basic exposition of the working of grace within human agency. I hope that this book will help young Christians to understand their emotions and integrate them within a spiritual life centered on Jesus Christ.

In my presentation of the human psyche, I follow the teachings of St. Thomas Aquinas. I first encountered this doctrine many years ago when I happened upon the writings of Anna A. Terruwe and Conrad Baars, two Dutch psychiatrists who saw the value of Thomistic psychology in clinical practice dealing with emotional disturbances. Readers of the works of these outstanding Catholic doctors will immediately note that I copiously repeat their insights in this book and also in other articles and books I have written. This is because I have seen the value of their explanations in clarifying the principles of moral theology and also in practical pastoral ministry. I am convinced, however, that what is to be said about the healthy functioning of the emotions has to be located within a presentation of the spiritual life open to grace. Hungering for happiness, engaging with God, living out charity, and dealing with oneself has to begin with a fascination with God, Who first has loved us, called us, and empowered us to go forward counting on His merciful grace. Thus, even though they are distinct, Christian spirituality, morality, and psychology overlap, and so the languages of theology and psychology have to be compatible.

I am grateful to Weronika Cichosz, who translated this book into English, and I also express my sincere thanks to Luanne Zurlo, who corrected the translation and made it more readable. I am thankful to the editors of EWTN, who prepared this publication in English. In doing so, they have followed the outline and the images used in the Polish edition, which was prepared by the publisher, my nephew Piotr Giertych, and his collaborator Beata Początek. I thank all these people, who now have made the English publication of this book possible.

Fr. Wojciech Giertych, O.P.

Preface

Of all sorts of shackles, are these—
Of rope, gold, or steel?…
—Most soaked with blood and tears…
I n v i s i b l e !

Cyprian Kamil Norwid

Feelings are captivating, and even more so, they can carry us away in such a manner that we sometimes find ourselves wondering afterward whether this is good or bad. Something has struck us, has us drawn in, has fascinated or outraged, upset or saddened us. Something that happened to us has had a beneficial, pleasant influence on our steps and decisions; or, on the contrary, it has provided strong sensations accompanied by inconstancy, mood swings, and general uncertainty, as a result of which we have, for some time, remained indecisive, without commitments, and sometimes in a state of sorrowful loneliness. Regardless of whether we judge this to be positive or negative, we know that the stirrings of feelings are our own, personal, and also sometimes temporary. We value them and are intrigued by them. Why do we perceive things in this manner? Why are we so inwardly moved?

There may sometimes be a fleeting desire for an anxiety to end swiftly, but the thought soon dawns on us that we do not want to be devoid of feelings. We do not want to be like dry wooden sticks or mechanical robots, obedient to the iron logic of a computer program. Feelings are part and parcel of our lives, and through them, we experience joy, warmth, and a fascinating thrill, and even when we are overcome by anger or sadness, we know that we are being real. Moreover, we are sensitive to the feelings of other people. They touch us, sometimes even more so than cold, rational arguments. Mutually expressed feelings, experienced and offered to others, create a bond and a closeness that we do not renounce, that we desire, knowing however, that it must be guarded.

It happens sometimes that feelings become wounded, and then they bring pain. When the expressed feeling is not reciprocated or, worse, is reciprocated but the reaction turns out to be illusory, false, and devoid of content, the experience of disappointment becomes a source of suffering. Reason can somehow explain it, but resentments linger in the psyche and hurt. And when feelings are fragile and sore, they are susceptible to addiction. It is easy for someone else to play on these restless emotions, and not necessarily in a way that we would like.

The ambition of this book, however, is not to speak of this. Its purpose is more modest. It merely seeks to name properly and explain the reality of the emotions. For centuries, people have been reflecting on the emotions and have finally developed a terminology precise enough to enable an exact articulation of the subject. The distinctions and definitions at use here do not provide moving literary descriptions. They are not a substitute for life, nor do they provide a simple home remedy for emotional wounds. They merely provide a skeleton: the essential elements of the human psyche, which are good to know and to understand properly. This can aid in developing a mature identity, free of painful anxieties. It is necessary, however, to live one's own life and not one according to recipes found in textbooks.

This book is a follow-up to my previous book on freedom. It is similarly aimed at youth, high school graduates and students who are reflecting upon their lives. If high school graduates can learn and use mathematics or physics, they can similarly familiarize themselves with the basic categories describing the human psyche. Mathematical knowledge does not remove freedom but, rather, enhances it and allows one to be more consistent and precise in one's calculations. Likewise, knowledge concerning the emotions does not extinguish them or root them out but can help in integrating a mature personality.

The emotional sphere, like the spiritual powers of reason and will, is the domain of the operation of divine grace. Communion with God, when consciously sustained in the soul, echoes throughout the whole person. Christian experience and orderly theological thought have something to say about this. I do not mention this divine influence parenthetically, as if I were ashamed of it. On the contrary, at the starting point of this explanation, I accept God's gift and try to identify its fruits in the psyche and in actions. Remaining in friendship with God bears effects also in the internal life of the human person.

It is worth knowing exactly what this means so as to avoid setting up conscious or unconscious barriers to God's power. God desires that we be whole and unharmed, freed from emotional entanglements, that we be true carriers of His love. He begs not only for our reason and our hands but also for our hearts — that is, for our smiles, our excitement, our fascination, and sometimes also our sadness and anger, for it is through cheeks inflamed with fervor and through gestures that something of God's goodness is disclosed. And even when we have some bodily, psychological, or intellectual inhibitions and limitations — which we all have — we can, in spite of them, accept, live, and share the gift of God's grace.

This is what this book is all about.

Wojciech Giertych, O.P.
Theologian of the Papal Household

I have come so that they may have life
and have it to the full.

John 10:10

I. What Are the Emotions?

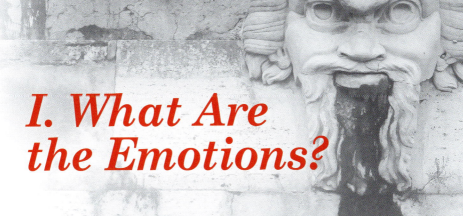

When speaking about emotions, we employ a variety of terms. We speak of feelings, passions, raptures, and desire, and these used to be called "affects." All of these terms are correct and, in some ways, interchangeable, although each points to a specific aspect of the emotions. Feelings always involve some kind of experienced movement, and therefore, compared with conscious active operations, the emotions are passive. They touch and carry us, taking us beyond the sphere we can precisely control. And it is good that they do so because they bring new, not always familiar experiences and impressions. They provide a little healthy madness that reminds us that we are alive. They add a warm, humane, and, at any rate, involved dimension to operations.

The emotions are rooted in the body. They move the body, making the face blush or blanch, cause tears to flow from the eyes, fascination and a smile to sparkle in the eyes, indignation to open the mouth, or astonishment to raise the eyebrows. Sexual excitement is also felt. In the emotions, a spontaneous reaction that is both bodily and psychic is manifested. It is not purely corporeal and is therefore different from the inner movement of the body, such as the beating of the heart, the circulation of the blood, the functioning of the lungs, or physical pain. The emotions also have a psychological dimension, touching on the spiritual powers, but they differ from the reason and the will. When we say "I want," we are engaging the spiritual powers, and when we say "I feel like," we are describing an emotional experience. However, our "I" is not the soul alone but the soul with the body. We are not purely spiritual beings — angels enclosed in corporeal machines. We are composed of both body and soul, which mutually influence one another and form one whole.

My soul is not I.

St. Thomas Aquinas

Animals also have feelings. They experience eagerness, pleasure, fear, and anger, but they do not have spiritual powers. Their emotional stirrings are always directed toward existing concrete realities. Humans, on the other hand, also recognize and desire general values and are able to relate their emotional movements to them.

Both animals and humans have an innate drive to preserve life and a sexual drive directed at transmitting it — that is, to preserve the species. Without any cognition or reflection on our part, something drives us to breathe, eat, drink, and avoid danger. Similarly, we have an innate sexual drive that is characterized by great strength. Emotions, however, emerge as a result of sensual apprehension. Something is perceived and instinctively liked or disliked, triggering an emotional experience that attracts or repels.

The strength of the emotions is not the same for everyone. Some people are cool-headed, while others are immediately affected by every issue, feeling a strong stirring within themselves. There is nothing wrong with this. Everyone has his or her own temperament, which is partly the result of the individual's somatic constitution and partly of very early experiences. Temperament is different from character. Temperament — that is, the power of emotional expression — is simply present and essentially unchangeable, whereas character is developed. A formed character means a permanent orientation of the personality toward values that are affirmed with one's whole being.

The ability to feel is a sign not of infantilism but of the fullness of humanity. It is true that children's feelings are more autonomous because they are as yet unformed, and therefore the child easily passes from one emotional state to another. Adults can usually handle their feelings, at least in part. If an adult suddenly jumps from crying to joy and vice versa, we think that this is abnormal, but it does happen to children.

Feelings are like the strings of a guitar; one is struck, and immediately the others reverberate too. Experienced feelings are transferred from person to person. The infant encounters affectionate love and responds with his or her own feeling. This is why it is good for the child to be emotionally loved, even before birth, and to feel, as an infant, the loving touch of both the mother and the father. This develops the capacity for emotional expression and attachment, which is a positive value. Adults also sense the feelings of others — especially those they love and those who love them — and it is good when they do not have to hide their feelings but can express them to one another. They then know that their feelings are not rejected, and therefore those individuals grow close to each other. Feelings can also pass from one to another in a crowd of strangers when they succumb to collective euphoria or panic.

In the passions, as movements of the sensitive appetite, there is neither moral good nor evil. But insofar as they engage reason and will, there is moral good or evil in them.

Catechism of the Catholic Church

The emotions, fundamentally, by the very fact that we naturally possess them, are good, all of them, including feelings of sadness, distaste, and anger. The question, however, is how do we deal with them? The residue of Original Sin and further sins of our own cause disorder in our emotions and sometimes lead us in undesired, unreasonable directions. It is therefore necessary to learn how to direct them within ourselves. This does not mean that we should negate their dynamics. Feelings should not be extinguished, nor should they be artificially stimulated. A man who is rigid, tied up, uncomfortable with his own feelings, and insensitive to others is abnormal, inhuman.

Emotions are dynamic. And it is good that they are such. We need, however, to be able to use their power well. In themselves, feelings are only an impulse, an internal motor or psychic spring that surges in a particular direction. They can be the fabric for a moral habit tending toward goodness, which we call virtue, but they can also be the fabric for vice. This multidirectionality of feelings explains why their terms are sometimes associated positively and at other times negatively. The feeling of anger, in itself, denotes an emotional reaction of indignation to evil, a reaction that is morally indifferent. This indignation can just as well serve fortitude in defending the good or be a source of unjust aggression. Similarly, the feeling of sadness can be the fabric for pity, which is part of mercy, and at other times, it may generate envy.

Of this concupiscence which the apostle occasionally calls "sin" […] the Catholic Church has never understood that it is called sin because it would be sin in the true and proper sense in those who have been reborn, but because it comes from sin and inclines to sin.

Council of Trent

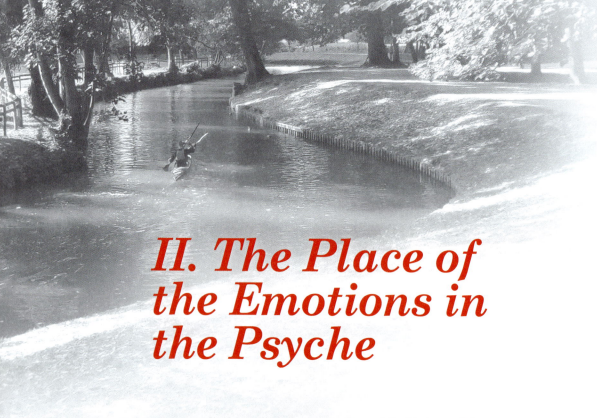

II. The Place of the Emotions in the Psyche

Emotions belong to the sensual sphere. We distinguish between cognitive senses, which grasp some content, and appetitive senses, which respond to that content.

We have five external cognitive senses: sight, hearing, smell, taste, and touch. All direct perceptions of the outside world are made by them. They use their own bodily organs, but they are not identified with them because the body may suffer an ailment. When Beethoven became deaf, he retained his inner sense of hearing and continued to compose, even though he was no longer able to hear his music.

Furthermore, there are four internal cognitive senses: common sense, memory, imagination, and the sensitive usefulness judgment. Common sense gathers together the perceptions of the external senses, forming from them one recognizable whole. Memory collects and stores content and experience.

Imagination extracts the stored impressions. It acts like active memory. The fourth internal cognitive sense is the sensitive usefulness judgment. It perceives the usefulness or harmfulness of what has been perceived by the external senses or invoked by memory and imagination. Animals instinctively grasp what is useful to them as food or for building a nest and what constitutes danger, and therefore this power in them has the character of evaluation (Latin: *vis aestimativa*). In humans, the sensitive usefulness judgment is intertwined with reason and is therefore marked by thinking (Latin: *vis cogitativa*).

The internal cognitive senses are developmental, susceptible to training. Reading fine literature or studying geometry cultivates the imagination. Some innately possess a perfect spatial imagination, while this comes with difficulty to others. The same is true of memory. It can be trained. Since animals likewise possess sensory powers, they are also susceptible to training. They accumulate experiences and can be drilled, that is, essentially manipulated by man.

Human sensory cognitive powers are connected to the mind. As a spiritual power, the mind reaches to the general meaning of things, and therefore, through it, individual facts perceived sensorially can be grasped in light of the universal. Humans can recognize and name melodies they hear and differentiate flavors of wine. Imagination, under the influence of the mind, may separate impressions and freely compile them; this is why it is capable of creativity. An animal is incapable of imagining mountains made of glass, but we humans can do so, even though we have never seen a glass mountain. The reflex of the human sensitive usefulness judgment may be guided by taking into account general values. Thanks to this instinctive judgment, both past and present experiences are immediately evaluated.

When objects are perceived sensorially, externally or internally, they trigger appropriate movements either toward or away from that which has been perceived. These movements are feelings, or emotions. They instinctively desire or turn away from a given object. A smell or a sound as well as a memory or the imagination can immediately provoke astonishment or a reflex of distaste or aversion.

The perceptions of the external senses brought together by the common sense and the imagination in unison perceive something as pleasant, attractive, or not. On the other hand, the sensitive usefulness judgment and the memory, recalling experiences, indicate the usefulness or harmfulness of the perceived object. As a consequence, there are two kinds of emotional response and so two distinct sets of emotions are distinguished: the urge to attain pleasure, also called the concupiscible appetite; and the urge to struggle, otherwise called the irascible appetite.

Emotions of the Concupiscible Appetite		Emotions of the Irascible Appetite	
Love (*amor*)	Hate (*odium*)	Hope or ambition (*spes*)	Courage (*audacia*)
Desire (*desiderium*)	Aversion (*fuga*)	Despair (*desperatio*)	Fear (*timor*)
Joy (*delectatio*)	Sadness (*tristitia*)		Anger (*ira*)

Figure 1. The emotions

The terms given here, both the Latin and the English, convey a fundamental, central theme in the emotional response. Of course, we can describe the matter more richly, more poetically, extracting further layers of the emotional movement, but, in the end, all feelings fit into the given terms. They do not mean any moral judgment because the mere feeling of emotions is morally neutral. Goodness or evil is born only as a result of the proper or inappropriate use of a given emotion. Therefore, the given term speaks not of the virtue of love but, rather, of the emotional drive to attain what is pleasant. Likewise, it is not sinful hatred that is named here but the response of reluctance that precedes conscious action. Similarly, the hope mentioned here does not constitute the theological virtue directed toward God but, rather, a response of zeal, giving strength to take a difficult step. Likewise, courage encompasses bravery or boldness, while anger expresses the very outrage against the known evil or threat.

Animals have the same set of feelings, and as with humans, their emotional reactions vary. One cat is swift in movement, and another cannot be bothered. One antelope will boldly jump over a stream, and the other will stop, as if despairing before the encountered difficulty.

The emotions of the concupiscible appetite respond to that which is pleasant or otherwise, while the emotions of the irascible appetite are characterized by assertiveness and optimism or express resistance. The latter serve to enable the emotions of the concupiscible appetite to attain their goal. Therefore, all the emotions of the urge to struggle are servile toward the pleasure appetite. When, in the desert, it turns out that the water supply is running out, the feelings of hope, despair, and even anger toward one's companions mobilize a person to move quickly toward an oasis, where there will be water and the thirst may be quenched with pleasure. Therefore, in the emotional life, primacy always belongs to the emotions of the concupiscible appetite. It is thanks to this set that a person is able to give and receive emotional warmth. When the irascible feelings prevail, emotional reactions become inhibited.

In animals, emotions induce autonomous movements. But humans, having spiritual powers, can consciously, through the reason and the will, accordingly choose actions that guide the feelings. This is not always easy because we are born with emotional disarray. This disarray is not, however, so strong as to render impossible the combination of the emotions and the spiritual powers. Furthermore, the emotions as well as the reason and the will are created, and thus they are inherently good, and their mutual cooperation is natural. In their structure, the emotions have a susceptibility to the light of reason, so combining them with reason is not only possible but also normal, not causing disturbances. When a doctor advises a diabetic to avoid sweets, at first it is difficult to adhere to the rule, but eventually the desire calmly receives the light of reason.

The sense appetite … was made to be moved by the reason.

St. Thomas Aquinas

In humans, the sensory powers and the spiritual powers are part of the same being, and therefore, there is no fundamental conflict between them. They can work together, but in order for them to do so, the individual occasionally has to play a little game with himself, for the power over the senses is "political" rather than "despotic." Knowing that something may be inappropriately tempting, one sometimes needs to consciously redirect the attention.

It is said that virtue lies in the mean. This does not mean that the enticement of alcohol ought not to be either too weak or too strong, but just right. The issue is that the action is to be reasonable, taking into account objective reasons, but the enjoyment of a given drink may be endless. The driver, in the name of justice, will refrain from drinking before driving the car, but he can still have the irresistible conviction and feeling that this brand of French cognac is really first-class!

*Excellence is a kind of mean,
since it aims at what is intermediate.*

Aristotle

When reason has determined the right measure, and it has been exceeded, then the emotion deprived of direction is uncomfortable. This gives rise to a feeling of guilt. It is not identical with the judgment of conscience because conscience is an act of reason — that is, of a spiritual power. But this does not change the fact that the feeling of guilt or satisfaction supports the judgment of conscience. The strength of this feeling depends on the disposition of the given individual. Some experience a strong sense of remorse, while others are colder. Therefore, the awareness of misconduct does not always imply a strong sense of guilt.

When discussing the emotions, the need for their mortification is sometimes mentioned. This term, "mortification," is unfortunate because it suggests that emotions should be made dead. This is not true! Nothing in us should be killed. All emotions are an integral and necessary part of the human psyche. Sometimes the strength of a feeling has to be curbed or, on the contrary, allowed to develop, but always in a reasonable manner, while affirming the essential goodness of the feeling. Mortification is most often associated with emotions of the pleasure appetite. Meanwhile, it happens that it is not these emotions that ought to be stopped but, rather, those of the irascible appetite — for example, the fear that gives rise to unhealthy scruples, or zeal that, when wrongly directed, causes internal psychological tension.

The contribution of the mind in directing the emotions consists not merely of inhibiting them or letting go. The mind cooperates with the emotional thrust and absorbs its strength, thus coming up with the correct expression. When we consider eating, it is not merely a question of finding the golden middle between anorexia and gluttony. The culture of eating values taste, allows itself to be carried away by invention, takes advantage of the experiences of other culinary traditions while taking temporal and financial constraints into account. Thanks to all of this, enjoying a meal is an opportunity for encounter and emotional connection. The same should be said of the remaining emotions. They are all the fabric of a mature, fully human life.

Virtue corrects the passions, but it also assumes them and holds them up.

Fr. Servais Pinckaers, O.P.

III. Faith Opening Up to Grace

Experiencing feelings and exercising faith are not the same thing. Participating in liturgies, especially when they are celebrated beautifully, in a historical church, with well-prepared music creates an uplifting atmosphere that is captivating to those who are present. Religious elation has a certain value because it moves the whole person, but not too great an importance should be attributed to it. The play of emotions, like all excitement, is momentary and fleeting, but one must move on in life. The strength of an emotional religious experience is by no means an indication of the quality of faith and of a real openness to the power of God.

It is possible to express faith, to remain in it and grow in it, even when one does not feel anything and, more so, when opposing feelings are experienced. One may be united to God by faith even when the church is cold, the singing is poor, and the sermon is boring and meaningless. Entrusting oneself to God and being united with Him are also possible while lying in a hospital bed and feeling pain, anxiety, or fatigue.

Faith is received at Baptism, or even earlier. It is a supernatural means that enables the coming into contact with God. At the moment of the expression of faith, the mind goes beyond the limits over which it has control and accepts as a gift the grace and truth received from God. This moment of humility of the mind, which is the act of faith, reaches far, even beyond concepts expressing salvific truth, and directly touches the living God Himself. And when God is touched by faith, He immediately imparts Himself. In the Gospels, Jesus always expects a trusting faith, and only when such a faith is present does a real encounter take place.

Your faith has restored you to health.

Mark 5:34

Thus, **faith expressed inwardly ignites the life of grace in us**. It is different from the life of the flesh, from sensual reactions and the intellectual life. The life of grace is of a completely different order because it is supernatural, but it is also not a distortion of that which is natural. Grace permeates and influences nature. In order for the power of God to work, however, a starting point is necessary; and that is the expression of faith.

God's giving Himself as a result of contact with the believer is something that is not felt. The moment of entrustment, in which one accepts God for Himself, is conscious. We know precisely when human arguments and purely rational reasons have been considered insufficient and we have dared, in spite of everything, to go on and to trust. Such moments are memorable. They also happen in interpersonal relationships, when we trust others, even strangers we meet on the street, and do not demand prior, empirically verified knowledge. We are all the more aware of situations in which even a momentary, instantaneous trust in God for Him alone has taken place.

The effects of such a trust are not immediately discernible, but if one makes a practice of allowing oneself and God the time to be with Him in faith, then, after a few months of regular personal prayer, one will become more open to Him in one's daily routine and that openness will become fruitful. This is why it is so important to make sure that time is set aside, every day, to remain with God in silent prayer. This does not have to be done in a church; it can be done at home, in the morning or the evening, or in the park during a break from work. What is important, however, is that this entrustment is genuine.

The life I now live in this body I live in faith: faith in the Son of God who loved me.

Galatians 2:20

God is touched not by thought or the senses but by faith. This is why it is not necessary before praying to wait until the feelings have calmed down and the mind is inwardly persuaded and ordered. The senses react on their own, often in a chaotic manner provoking emotional excitement. The mind can become distracted, jumping from one topic to another. Some experience pains and resentments, or plans may rattle around in the head. The memory of one's follies and sins is unsettling, and all these things resonate in the psyche.

This does not mean, however, that one cannot or should not pray in these moments. It is precisely in the midst of this chaos that one can try to use the received faith, which is already infused in the soul, and express it inwardly. It is at this point that contact with God is made.

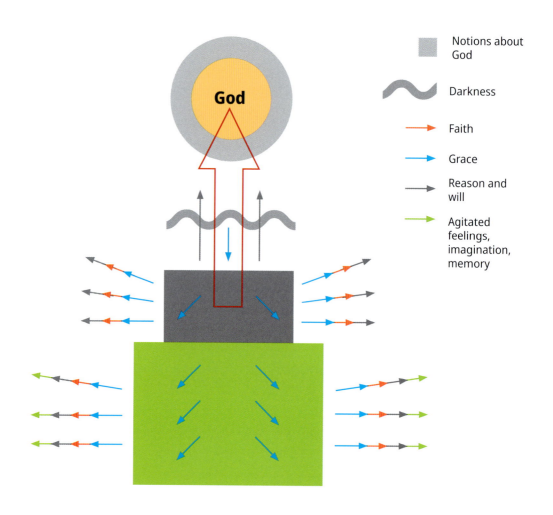

Figure 2. God is touched in prayer by faith, not through thinking or by the senses. Grace, set in motion, eventually orders the senses.

Grace communicated at the moment of an internal expression of faith is like an underground stream, invisible, hidden in the soul, but real. When perseverance in faith becomes regular, when moments dedicated to it are prolonged, when we learn not to worry too much about emotions and thoughts in order to stay with God, this invisible stream of grace will begin to irrigate the soul. From within, not by our own efforts but by the power of God and according to the steady divine timetable, a gradual healing of the psyche, of action, and of life will begin. Difficulties will be resolved. Ideas for life and a readiness to take risks will appear. Old sins will cease to trigger panic and an ease in mature, responsible love will come.

Holiness ... is an encounter between your weakness and the power of God's grace.

Pope Francis

It is possible to grow in faith, but this is not done by expanding one's knowledge, even religious knowledge. Learning based on the *Catechism* has its value because it locates the received divine truths in the mind and facilitates trust, but faith, in its essence, grows when it is renewed in prayer and applied to life. Faith is nourished by the Word of God, the truths of faith, and the reception of the sacraments, but it grows when one courageously and at the same time confidently takes the steps suggested by God Himself. "Everyone moved by the Spirit is a son of God" (Rom. 8:14). Sensitivity to divine suggestions bestows a childlike serenity and joy before God and, at the same time, makes it possible to be authentic and responsible in the face of life's challenges.

It is said, it is much sweeter to give than to receive, and it is true. But when Jesus wills to take for Himself the sweetness of giving, it would not be gracious to refuse.

St. Thérèse of Lisieux

The fruits of grace present in the soul appear gradually, and we should not be alarmed that we are not immediately rendered perfect. In prayer, we rely on God, counting on His power, which will come when it comes. Before this happens, often experiencing our own powerlessness, we can believe and continue to wait. It is important, however, to express faith in this and to do so often, both in moments of planned prayer and during the day in the midst of various activities. It is also important to **believe in the supernatural character of the expressed faith**. It has been given to us in order to be used. It is a tool, a means of encountering God. And by relying on God, Who is mysterious and intriguing but real, we have a firm foundation that allows us to move forward with courage.

IV. Faith Is Followed Up with Hope and Charity

Faith comes first. When inwardly expressed, it ignites the life of grace in the soul, and then hope and charity follow. These are the theological virtues — the habits, received at Baptism, that come from God and lead to Him. These virtues, too, can be ignored, but they can also be used consciously and developed in such a way that, over time, they take hold of the whole psyche, opening it up to the power of God.

The theological virtue of hope differs from both the emotion and the natural virtue of hope. The emotion of hope, or healthy ambition, is a sensory psychic dynamic experienced also by animals. This feeling of hope provides the eagerness for undertaking difficult tasks. It is the fabric of both good and evil abilities. Someone with a feeble emotion of hope will never rob a bank — above all because he quite simply cannot be bothered to do so! Together with goodwill, this emotion forms the natural virtue of hope, sometimes called magnanimity. It directs us to the issues of this world and prompts us to deal with them. That is why we say that hope gives the strength to act. It is very necessary in life. Those who succumb to depression and constant discouragement will not achieve anything in their lives and will constantly search for some means of fulfillment that will artificially fill the void.

There is a similarity between the natural virtue of hope and theological hope, but there also is a difference between them, due to the higher order of the theological virtue. Theological hope is located not in the emotions but in the will, which it then directs toward God and toward that divine mystery that, step by step, unfolds itself throughout life. We do not have a special terminology to describe the impulses of the will and even less to describe the power of grace, so we transfer words referring to feelings to the spiritual reality. Theological hope is concerned with God and not some current success or emotional experience. He who hopes in God endures difficulties, does not break down, and, what is more, trusts in the hand of God, which guides him. He does not proudly dictate anything to God, and he knows how to set aside memories, good or bad, so that they do not block him and so he is ready to accept the surprises that God places in his path.

This hope follows faith and pushes even further, leading one toward charity. You cannot place your hope in God if you do not believe in Him, and you cannot love God if you are not moving toward Him. The Polish language has no special term for supernatural love. Other languages are richer in this respect (Latin: *caritas*; English: *charity*). Like theological faith and hope, charity is a gift of grace, received at Baptism and renewed in the sacraments. It enables one to enter into a friendship with God and then to transfer this friendship to others. He who loves God discovers that he has been drawn into the community of His friends. When we love a friend, we also have a special relationship with his friends and family. Likewise, when we love God, we also love people for His sake because they, too, are loved by Him.

God is faithful, by whom you were called into the fellowship of his Son, Jesus Christ our Lord.

1 Corinthians 1:9

In friendship, there is a relatively equal level between the friends. We can enter into a serious friendship only with a person, and not with a puppy, although an animal can provide a great deal of emotional warmth. Furthermore, in friendship, there are present a common goal and an exchange of goods that lead to it. These elements unite and express friendship. Hence, it is worth looking into the common goal of each friendship. What is it that unites friends? Is it a mere chance encounter resulting from fate? Or are there serious values and goals that are worth committing to together? In friendship, there is giving and receiving, but when you give, for example, an ice cream, which can be an expression of kindness, it is clear that friendship refers to something deeper, more serious. So what is friendship about when we want it to be real?

There is an infinite gap between us and God, but we can love Him because He has elevated us, by grace, to His own level. Even more, He has revealed to us the common goal of remaining with Him in a communion of friendship that shall last eternally but begins now. With God, we can, like a child, share the affairs, secrets, joys, and troubles of our everyday lives. When we think about it, it seems otherworldly, inconceivable, but can we conceive of a perspective that would give greater happiness?

The love of God has been poured into our hearts by the Holy Spirit which has been given us.

Romans 5:5

We can transfer the adventure of communing with God to others. We can love people for the sake of God. When we love someone with the love of God, we want that loved one not only to enjoy our ice cream and express gratitude, and not simply to be with us; above all, we want him or her to become a better person, to participate also in trusting union with God, and to enjoy the deepest spiritual bond.

When we love God, we do not treat Him as an enemy Who only commands and forbids. We see in Him a Father Who bestows love, and so, in turn, we wish to give something of ourselves to Him, for no other reason than to please Him. When charity grows and finally prevails in the soul, it may be playful toward God. Instead of cold seriousness or fear, a joyful communing takes place. This is because, in all true love — whether toward a loved one or, even more so, toward God — a corner of the soul is disclosed to the other, in which something of the child still remains. In simplicity, one asks for help in all one's needs, even trivial ones, and willingly gives one's childlike gifts.

Your Love has gone before me,
and it has grown with me, and now it is an abyss
whose depths I cannot fathom.

St. Thérèse of Lisieux

It is important for us to know that it is possible to love God like a child and that we may struggle to ensure that this bond is fundamental in life. It is not something we have from ourselves or can produce in ourselves.

That we can connect with God is a consequence of the fact that at Baptism we have received the three virtues of faith, hope, and charity and that they are renewed whenever we receive sacramental absolution. These virtues are already installed in the soul, and retrieving this supernatural program so that it may appear on the screen of our consciousness is not difficult. When we use these capacities to connect with the living God, invoking Him and His power becomes simple and automatic.

We should not think that we have to be perfect and without sin in order to approach God. This view is false and keeps us tied down. Let us learn from children. Silly things happen to them, yet they are able to love because they know and feel that they are loved. Adults, however, often find this difficult. They cannot or do not know that it is possible to be childlike before God, and so they needlessly exaggerate the drama of their sins and force themselves into seriousness, which poisons the relationship. Meanwhile, it is most important to befriend God by living out faith, hope, and charity, directed toward Him, in simplicity. From this, in time, a relative moral order and a certain psychic order will emerge, but this is not the most important issue.

Matthew … not only gave a banquet for the Lord at his earthly residence, but far more pleasing was the banquet set in his own heart which he provided through faith and love.

Venerable Bede

It is a terrible mistake foolishly to think that we must first bring ourselves to an immaculate, perfect state by our own efforts and that a relationship with God is a matter for distant old age. That is nonsense!

V. Emotional Difficulties

We all find ourselves wondering, from time to time, why we reacted in a particular way in a given situation, why we allowed ourselves to be carried away by emotions and to act foolishly. Because feelings are bodily, they are experienced passively. Something happens in us, and sometimes we lack the inner freedom or ability to control this and to direct our reactions toward the goals we truly wish to achieve. Is it possible ever to come to terms with ourselves?

We hear about faith, about communing with God, but it all seems to be distant, very theoretical. Faith is not felt; feelings, on the contrary, *are* felt and sometimes very strongly, especially when they are hurt or out of place. Their distortion makes itself known at once because it can be painful. It is like an injury or a bodily disorder that immediately signals its presence with pain.

When the emotions function correctly and are properly directed, they do not cause any trouble. They add fervor and zeal to what is being done. Thanks to them, reactions are fully human, engaged. Emotional states are not then a source of anxiety, and in a moment of reflection, they are assessed well.

It is true that the emotions draw us in part into the unknown, but thanks to them, life has flavor. The ability to make a conscious, free choice — that is, to take control of ourselves — is not then lost because it presupposes and accepts that feelings sometimes drag us in a direction determined by their surges.

Emotional swings, on the other hand, chain us and therefore are tormenting. They are various. It is considerably easier to spot serious mental disorders because their symptoms are much more glaring. In turn, slight emotional disparities may be shallow and fundamentally harmless, but they can bring about restlessness and cause the individual to feel awkward. We feel uncomfortable when our emotions are unhinged or, on the contrary, blocked and therefore sore. Emotions that are out of tune, akin to an untuned piano string, produce a painful rasp every time they are struck. In reaching maturity, one must be able to deal with one's emotional sphere in such a way that it does not hinder life but, rather, aids in it.

Those who did not experience warmth in childhood oftentimes experience a deep emotional hunger in their adult lives. An infant is loved and touched lovingly not because he has done something but simply because he is there. But somebody who grew up in an orphanage or in a family in which the parents were quarrelsome, self-involved, or busy making money and had no interest in the children often experiences a lack of warmth. Such individuals, in their adult lives, constantly crave affection and contact from people close to them. Because such people perceive emotions like a child, they become egocentric and are only able to respond when others direct their feelings toward them; they are incapable of establishing emotional contact themselves. Such people feel set aside. They have acquaintances but no friends. Sometimes they even think that this is a good thing, and they run away from others, closing themselves off. They prefer work that does not require contact with people. They prefer to be archivists rather than teachers. Their marriages are difficult because the wife unconsciously looks for a father in her husband, while the husband tries to find a mother in his wife. Others, on the other hand, can be very active, successful, take on positions of leadership, but at the heart of everything they do is a constant craving for appreciation and applause. They cannot tell the difference between what was said seriously and a witty remark made in jest, because they are always oversensitive about their own person.

People suffering from such a deprivation neurosis can be helped only when they are drawn into a safe space of sympathetic people, capable of providing trust and affirmation. Only when they feel that they are valued not because of what they do but simply because they exist and have meaning as a person do they experience a kind of rebirth, an emotional discovery of their own worth. They then become more stable and balanced.

A much more serious disorder is the psychopathic state, in which there is a fundamental split between the rational and sensory spheres. The psychopath can be rational to the bone, but he feels nothing. When he does wrong, he understands and knows that he will suffer consequences for his actions, but he feels absolutely no guilt because he does not feel anything at all. He is therefore also completely insensitive to the feelings of other people. He simply does not care about them. This condition is a deep disorder, extremely difficult to treat.

In neurotics, the emotions are fundamentally sound. They have an intrinsic need for cooperation with the reason and the will, but as a result of a faulty approach and upbringing, their emotions are mutually blocked. This instinctive habit causes psychic tension and an inability to curb certain unwanted emotional stirrings. The neurotic person can be fully normal in many areas of his life while remaining internally enslaved in one field. In this disturbed area, something will push him into embarrassing actions that cannot be controlled. Since the emotions of the neurotic are fundamentally sound, once a correction of the improper reflexes takes place in the psyche, emotional equilibrium returns.

It is important to be able to distinguish between a normal directing of the emotions and their neurotic repression because this affects the moral and spiritual life. A healthy approach to emotions directs them in such a way that they are elevated and transformed by the spiritual influence of reason and will — that is, of conscious choices. Feelings then serve the purpose of human expression. When a person is a believer and, moreover, strives to live the charity received in grace, feelings become the means through which something of God's love is disclosed. On the other hand, someone who sins with the senses but whose approach to the emotional sphere is well formed consciously allows the feelings to exceed the proper measure that has been recognized by reason. Consequently, the individual knows that he could have acted differently but that he chose what is inappropriate, and so he evaluates his actions negatively and simultaneously feels guilty about them.

It is important, therefore, that the reception of moral indications be rational, and not emotional, because then the undertaken action takes into account the value that in itself is attractive, whereas the fact that the instruction also speaks of it is secondary. Whereas if the emotional reaction to the one who instructs by issuing orders and prohibitions is more significant, and the content of the instruction and its value are not understood or are considered to be irrelevant, this gives rise to unhealthy chaos in the emotions.

A defective attitude toward the emotions generates a fragile psychic terrain, on which sprout mood swings, aimlessness, anxiety, constant doubts, postponement of committed decisions, offense, frustrations, resentments, and grudges toward others, as well as compulsive neurotic tendencies, which are the source of inveterate actions and, finally, addictions. Someone with a fragile, insecure emotionality can easily succumb to the powerful pressure of a stronger individual who is not necessarily honest in everything. He or she may then become a victim of abuse, selfish demands, manipulation, threats, and even sexual deviance. It is also against such a background that mafia dependencies and submission to dictators are born.

The man lived in the tombs and no one could secure him any more, even with a chain; because he had often been secured with fetters and chains but had snapped the chains and broken the fetters, and no one had the strength to control him. All night and all day, among the tombs and in the mountains, he would howl and gash himself with stones.... They came to Jesus and saw the demoniac sitting there, clothed and in his full senses.

Mark 5:3–5, 15

People with fragile emotional lives, unsure of themselves and their identity and experiencing a deep loneliness with which they cannot cope, often succumb to persons who attract them with their charm, determination, and strength of psyche. When these persons are balanced, of true spiritual and moral worth, they are able to draw the weak toward the good and help them to acquire inner stability, and in this they do not make the weak dependent on them. If, however, the demand for such dependence were to begin to emerge, it would be a sign for the weak to break away and courageously go his or her own way. Authentic spiritual directors do not bind others to themselves but lead others toward God, and then they let go of the ones they have led. Normal parents do the same. They rejoice when their children grow up and go out into the world, into their own lives. It is only immature mothers who want to hold on to their grown-up children, thus doing them harm.

Ephata, ephata, open up! Lord, heal me.
Lord, make me dance for You!
Ephata, ephata, open up!

O Unfathomable Trinity Hymnal

VI. Attempts at Dealing with the Emotions

Basically, there are three ways of dealing with emotional swings. It is good to know this and to be able to differentiate between them, at least theoretically. The practical grasping of one's inner approach requires a certain capacity for introspection. Not everyone, especially the young person, is able to examine himself carefully. Only life experience allows one to better see and understand what goes on in the psyche.

Differentiating the three approaches to emotions, like any theoretical reflection, captures the essential contours of reality. In practice, there is often an unconscious sliding from one method into another. At one time, one approach to feelings may prevail, and at a different time, another. This is why coming to know these methods theoretically allows for a better insight into one's inner self; this can be useful, especially when anxieties arise and chaos reigns in the psyche.

The first method is supernatural. It is based on a bond with God, sustained in the soul by an active faith, followed by hope and charity. Of course, this active faith is not necessarily incessant. There may be stops and interruptions in attentiveness to God. This is not a bad thing, provided that the intervals are followed by returns and eventually God is sought after and consciously loved. Thus, when, in practice, God becomes most important, numerous moral virtues, stemming from grace follow the theological virtues. These moral virtues order the reason and the will as well as the emotional sphere from within in their relation not to God but to a variety of ordinary matters. Traditional theology states that the moral virtues, given by grace, for those who live them, make it easy, quick, and pleasant to do the good. To this we can add that there also occurs a moment of creativity in choosing the proper good. It is not a question of following a preordained program. On the contrary, the one who is open to grace is inwardly free and does the good because he wants to and often does so in an interesting and innovative way, according to personal discernment.

Cut off from me you can do nothing.

John 15:5

This is how traditional theology puts it, but life experience shows that this does not happen automatically. First of all, the relationship with God must be sustained and developed by repeated internal acts of faith and charity. The quality of one's personal, childlike relationship with God must be fought for. Moreover, there occasionally arise inner resistances in the psyche, and these make it difficult to develop proficiency in dealing with one's feelings.

This will also have to be discussed because even when one trusts in God, one sometimes has to face these obstacles.

The second approach to feelings is not supernatural but natural. It seems to be the most obvious one. The emotions must be governed, and the power that does this is the will. Together with reason, the will chooses the good, and it reigns over the feelings in its name. This method may seem straightforward and obvious, but experience shows that it is not, in fact, an unproblematic path. Can willpower, which is, after all, a spiritual power, grow? If so, what must one do to be strong-willed? Working on oneself by one's own efforts often turns out to be ineffective and essentially prideful. When the limits of self-sufficiency are exposed, this helplessness can be painful.

The third approach is the attempt to repress uncomfortable feelings, done by force, by the power of other feelings. Such emotional entanglement is unhealthy. This is the very essence of neurosis, which gives rise to compulsive symptoms. The individual tries to push the unwanted emotion out of the psyche, but it resurfaces and becomes increasingly more disturbing. Most commonly, at least initially, this is done unconsciously.

Trying to control one's feelings by will alone and, even more so, slipping into neurotic reactions, is often the result of running away from God, not always consciously. There is something frightening about communing with and trusting in God that men in particular are afraid of. The Gospel shows us St. Joseph and St. Peter, who were frightened by God's adventure and wanted to run away from it because they were convinced that it was not for them. The temptation to do things our own way, by our own power, through mechanisms we have developed on our own, in the belief that we will be able to control ourselves, is very strong. Trusting in God, on the other hand, is mysterious and seems to be as uncertain as walking on water!

The child ... is alone in a little boat; the land has disappeared from her eyes, she does not know where she is going, whether she is advancing or if she is going backward.... The rudder ... is not without a pilot. Jesus is there, sleeping, as in the days gone by, in the boat of the fishermen of Galilee.... However if He were to awaken only for an instant, He would have only to command the wind and the sea, and there would be a great calm.

St. Thérèse of Lisieux

There is one more, a fourth method of approaching feelings, that should not be underestimated, and that is a sense of humor about oneself. Feelings lead off into the unknown and draw us in, and as a result, we often make mistakes. Is that not amusing? Not everything we do has to be taken seriously. Emotional stirrings bring fantasy, create funny situations, and expose the carnal, even animal, part of our being. When we do not take ourselves too seriously, we do not panic when things do not go the way our calculated reason would like them to. Giving in to emotional impulses, not always rational, is also a part of our experience. Blessed are those who can laugh at themselves, for they will have fun all their lives!

Placed at the service of freedom, humor is its guarantor and makes it joyful. One can almost say: where there is no humor, there is neither freedom nor virtue.

Fr. Servais Pinckaers, O.P.

VII. Grace Within the Emotions

Dealing with emotional difficulties is not the goal of the spiritual life. Its goal is a bond of friendship with God. Only as a result of the action of grace does a gradual arrangement of the internal psyche occur. Whoever subordinates prayer and the reception of the sacraments to the demand that something be accomplished immediately that would free one from specifically indicated difficulties reduces God to the rank of means that can be used. This is an imposing of one's plan upon God.

We should not be too surprised that such a reflex arises from time to time. The fact that we express our worries and requests in prayer is completely normal and legitimate, but at the same time, we have to accept that in our friendship with God, He is the leading figure. Therefore, the time and means for the resolution of our difficulties is a matter for God and we cannot rush this. God sometimes deliberately leaves some "thorn in the flesh" (2 Cor. 12:7), some disturbing difficulty or weakness, and this teaches us to lean more profoundly on Him alone. It may take years to free ourselves from inner resistances that block the emotions at a certain point and even unconsciously prevent us from allowing grace into those corners of the psyche, especially when the incorrect mechanisms have become chronic. But the deeper and more trustful our relationship with God — which is, as it were, a transferring of the problem onto the shoulders of Christ, leaving it to Him to decide about the solution — the more His power works within us.

So we observe a certain disorder in ourselves. Emotions draw us and steer in different directions, and sometimes this is not particularly wise. As a consequence of Original Sin and our own sins, as well as under the influence of the environment in which we find ourselves, we experience a partial chaos. Few people always function smoothly and efficiently. Some roughness appears in everyone, but the relationship with God gradually smooths this out and makes the disorder disappear.

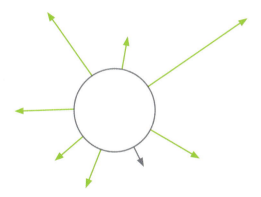

Figure 3. Compelling and disordered tendencies

When communion with God through faith, consciously expressed internally in moments of prayer, is placed at the forefront of the psyche and of life, followed by hope in and love of God, this central axis sets the whole life. God, touched by a living faith, immediately communicates Himself because this is the inner need of God Himself, who wants to bestow His love upon us. Grace, mysterious and invisible but real, permeates, then, the whole of the human personality. The good deeds that are then performed have something of the power of God in them. They may seem trivial, like the proverbial giving of a glass of water, but in these gestures, the goodness of God Himself is manifested and sometimes noticed. People are then grateful not so much to us as to God, who has touched them through our gesture.

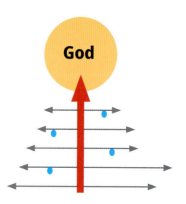

Figure 4. Tendencies ordered around the axis of a living faith

This does not mean, however, that God only externally adorns us with His power. He works within our generosity. Our deeds, together with their emotional involvement are our own, and in them, the goodness of God Himself is manifested! When we associate the above diagram with a spruce tree, it is important to emphasize that the good deeds that grow out of grace are more like pinecones and not Christmas tree ornaments. God works within individuals who are united to Him, and, at the same time, He does not manipulate them; He does not treat them as if they were lifeless agents in His hand. God alone can work within us in this way. Our entire personality, including our will and our living, bodily feelings, have their dignity and value in the eyes of God. God needs our generosity, our hands, our tears, our smiles, our impetus and enthusiasm, in fact, all of our emotions and drives so that through them, here and now, His goodness may manifest itself.

To be moved by the prompting of God ... is in accord with the nature of all man's faculties.

St. Thomas Aquinas

In the illustration, one branch sticks out and is without fruit; this does not mean that the remaining branches lack cones. Some weaknesses and emotional difficulties remain; nevertheless, it is possible to do good, counting on the full support of God. We should not, therefore, concentrate on our emotional wounds and difficulties because, by relying on God, we can already consciously and courageously do the good. In this manner, we can come out of being stuck on ourselves.

God sometimes permits his elect to be prevented by something on their part, e.g., infirmity or some other defect, and sometimes even mortal sin.... Thus ... they may recognize that they cannot stand by their own powers.

St. Thomas Aquinas

The process described here points to an important principle: **We must first take care of the theological virtues — that is, communion with God — rather than the moral virtues.** We need thus to free ourselves from erroneous thinking that suggests that we cannot approach God if we have repeated sins on our consciences. Everybody has some weaknesses and frequently experiences a disorder in the feelings, but already it is possible to unite with God by responding to His love through our own modest gestures.

When we do what is good, even if it is something minute, such as offering a kind smile to an unpleasant person, we do not consider ourselves to be doing a great thing, fulfilling some duty, or bringing order into our ill feelings. That is not what is significant at the time. But by remembering God, we can invoke His power through faith, asking that this smile, this contact with the other person, will have something of divine love in it. There is then a certain playfulness in this approach to God because the human gesture, hands, creativity, and feelings are given to Him, for His pleasure, so that He, at this very moment, may have the joy of manifesting His goodness.

Fresh altar-roses, Lord, / are gratified to shine —
Self-gifts we see! — / Instead of that I would
(this other dream is mine) / Un-petal me.

St. Thérèse of Lisieux

It is possible to be friendly with God, like a child, trusting in His presence, responding to His suggestions, and putting oneself at His disposal. "Everyone moved by the Spirit is a son of God" (Rom. 8:14). When one remains in faith, deepening it in silent prayer, sensitivity to divine whisperings and readiness to respond to them grow — out of love, quickly and for the joy of God alone.

When Jesus is exalted by faith, He draws all things to Himself (see John 12:32) and the wounded parts of the psyche, including the feelings, are healed from within. The capacities to act well, that is, the moral virtues, which refer to things of everyday life, are then developed easily, without the need for heroic effort. Therefore, when we experience a moral difficulty, even a recurring one, we should not panic; it is enough if the impulse of faith and charity leads to God and the first step is undertaken. It will be followed by others, and slowly a profound change will come about. But this change is not the goal. It is not about our being able to adore and praise ourselves for how well things are going in life for us right now. The point is that we remain in friendship with God.

You make me think of a little child that is just learning to stand but does not yet know how to walk. In his desire to reach the top of the stairs to find his mother, he lifts his little foot to climb the first step. It is all in vain, and at each renewed effort he falls. Well, be like that little child. Always keep lifting your foot to climb the ladder of holiness, and do not imagine that you can mount even the first step. All God asks of you is good will. From the top of the ladder, He looks lovingly upon you, and soon touched by your fruitless efforts, He will Himself come down, and, taking you in His arms, will carry you to His kingdom never again to leave Him.

St. Thérèse of Lisieux

We should seek God more than psychic order, emotional balance, or moral perfection. Whereas, when one runs away from God, then various difficulties arise, including emotional ones.

VIII. Emotions Directed by the Will

A living bond with God through faith is not necessary for directing the emotions. They can be controlled in an entirely natural manner. The human senses, unlike the animal, are innately susceptible to collaboration with the spiritual powers of reason and will, and therefore the ability to harmonize them can be acquired to a certain extent through education and training. In order to achieve this, it is sometimes necessary to take a "political, but not despotic" approach to oneself, avoiding explosive situations, but this is possible and entirely healthy.

*The intellect rules the appetites
with a constitutional and royal rule.*

Aristotle

When we think about it, we are more likely to pay attention to the will than to reason, but, in fact, the two powers function together. Free choice is directed toward something that has been perceived and evaluated and, as such, is wanted. At the same time, the emotions become involved and sometimes even take the initiative, and this is most often done in a controlled manner.

Fascination, enthusiasm, hope or joy, and sometimes even anger add their contribution. Anger is also important because in order to achieve something, to stand for something, at times it is necessary to get angry, and then adrenaline adds bodily strength to the action. Of course, all of this happens in the blink of an eye.

The moral value of an action is not necessarily reflected in the emotions. It is possible to pursue an evil goal, knowing it to be wicked, and have the feelings completely subordinated. One who commits crimes "in cold blood" keeps his emotions in check so that they do not interfere. It is different in the case of one who sins out of weakness because he then feels guilty and experiences unease.

Taking a closer look at the relationship between the reason, the will, and the emotions allows one to grasp more precisely the specificity of those virtues that bring order to the feelings. They reside not in the will but in the emotion itself, which can be directed by the spiritual powers. Thus, for example, in sobriety, it is not the will by its strength that subdues the rogue desire for alcohol because, within this desire, there is already a susceptibility to rational direction. The sober person calmly adapts to the rational measure, all the while not losing the taste for the good wine. The virtues that cover the sensual sphere are an expression of self-control, which is easy, quick, pleasant, and even creative in finding the proper response. This ease is the result of the internal susceptibility of the emotions to the influence of the rational desire and the acquired skill.

This, of course, is the case when there is a genuine harmonization of the emotions with the world of recognized and desired values. Even when, in a particular area of life, there is still disorder and missteps occur due to a strong emotional dynamic that manifests itself beyond measure and does not allow itself to be directed by free choice, in other areas there may be correct and easy control. Someone may have difficulties in the sexual area and not be able to experience it in a chaste way but, at the same time, in most cases, may easily and even spontaneously control anger or sadness.

That said, it is necessary to **distinguish the inner, virtuous harmonization of the emotions from the attempt to tame them through sheer willpower**. Such a reflex also occasionally occurs. In this case, there is as yet no internal ordering of the emotion but only the involvement of the will, which, with its spiritual power, restrains the disobedient feeling. The will then, in sudden necessity, like an emergency brake, temporarily holds the rebellious emotion in check. Consequently, the person does not succumb to a strong temptation, does not commit sin, but the whole experience is an expression of inner stress and struggle. In this case, the emotion is not domesticated; it is not accustomed to react calmly and appropriately, and so it persists in agitation until the occasion of falling has passed, and all the time, it is held back by the will.

Relating this mechanism to sexual desire, ethics calls it continence (Latin: *continentia*). It has something of virtue in it, because the sexual desire is ultimately restrained in the name of honesty, but not completely because the unbridled arousal continues, just as it happens in impurity. Continence, therefore, is solely in the will, following the rationale of reason, but it finds no support from the drive itself, which it fights by resisting it.

This is entirely different in the case of the virtue of chastity. For a chaste person, finding the right expression of affection that respects the dignity and the personal and bodily integrity of the other comes spontaneously because sexual feelings are ordered and domesticated. This does not mean that they have been cut out. At the right moment, as in the conjugal act, they will unveil themselves with their full natural dynamic. It is therefore one internal experience when everything depends on sheer willpower and a different one when the will does not have to exert itself because the feeling itself cooperates with the free choice and is accustomed to find release only in appropriate situations.

A similar phenomenon occurs with perseverance, which is also not a true virtue. It is a dynamic of the will that resists one emotion and stimulates another, as it were, from the outside, with the result being that one continues the required activity. The emotions, however, persist in dissatisfaction and resistance. An efficient impulse to work is different. The artist, scientist, or skilled craftsman does not need to force himself because the work itself fascinates and is attractive. At most, what is needed is the putting aside of distractions. That is why applying oneself to work (Latin: *studiositas*) is a virtue allied with the cardinal virtue of temperance and not fortitude.

Continence, desisting from pleasures, and perseverance in the midst of sadness are not full virtues, but rather less than a virtue.

St. Thomas Aquinas

Developing natural, acquired virtues that accommodate the emotions is not impossible, but neither is it easy or obvious. At times, relying on willpower alone will win out, but this brings stress and constant tension in relating to the emotions. A psyche internally structured in this manner generates a tense, serious, we would say "hard-headed" personality, more focused on the evil it wants to avoid than on the good that is worth undertaking for the sake of joy and pleasure alone. The building of moral excellence solely through training and self-control is most often accompanied by pride.

People who understand the moral duty of dealing with their emotions in this way often seek external support in protective customs and environments. Particularly those who have grown up among emotional chaos and relativistic confusion often turn to religious communities that provide them with a kind of psychic armor that offers protection against dangerous emotional outbursts. This need may be temporary, and after a period of psychic grounding and the establishment of an internal moral order, and especially after the deepening of faith and friendship with God, they leave these communities.

Self-mastery solely through natural willpower is dominant in the Muslim approach. Islam does not know of grace or of an interpersonal relationship with God through faith and love. It has only religiosity with obedient worship owed to God and submission to a simple morality adapted to purely natural possibilities and protected by very strict, socially prescribed rules with regard to dress and behavior. This is why, in Islamic ethics, the externally imposed law is at the center and there is no cultivation of personal virtues and personalism.

In the "Religion of Reason" conscience excites merely shame, when the mind is simply angry with itself and nothing more.... Self-reproach is directed and limited to our mere sense of what is fitting and becoming.

St. John Henry Newman

A strict upbringing based exclusively on willpower is psychologically difficult to bear. Hence, it often generates extreme reactions, either aggressive, enraged insistence on one's own rules or, on the contrary, the desire for a stress-free upbringing without any requirements. This, of course, is even worse because it lets the emotions loose, and this, in time, leads astray.

A life of faith, which allows supernatural power into the psyche, is completely different. Then one does not have to be a cold, serious ascetic. He who, like a child, remains in union with God also has to learn how to control himself, but his asceticism is mystical, based on trust in the accompanying help of God. This is expressed in a playful generosity, capable of pleasing God and others. Unrepressed emotions have an irreplaceable role in this.

IX. Blocked Emotions

An untamed emotion generates anxiety. As a result, sometimes an unhealthy neurotic mechanism appears, in which one emotion comes into conflict with another and tries to drive it out of the psyche. Two emotions then direct themselves simultaneously to the same object. This is not the phenomenon of mixed feelings, in which one feeling follows another. One may have mixed feelings of sadness and joy, for example, after the death of an unpleasant mother-in-law. On the one hand, there is sadness caused by the death, and on the other, there is a feeling of relief and joy that life may now be easier. The phenomenon of mixed feelings may irritate, but it is not a psychic disorder.

A classic example of a neurotic reflex is when a sexual feeling naturally arises, and simultaneously fear appears, alarmed by the drive, and then it tries to push it out of the psyche. This mechanism is unhealthy and causes a state of tension. It differs from directing the emotions by free choice. Restraining the expression of desire out of respect for the other person and the truth about him or her is reasonable and peaceful, but it does not negate the natural reaction of sexuality. It may be accompanied by fascination because the other person is indeed attractive and charming, but ultimately the spiritual powers decide. In the neurotic approach, however, it is not reason and will that are decisive but a feeling of fear, perceiving the urge as something inappropriate and threatening. Thus, this is not the action of conscience, which is an act of reason and influences the will, but of fear, which attempts to deal with the undesired urge.

In the neurotic mechanism, most often there is a conflict between emotions belonging to the two groups (the concupiscible and the irascible appetites). In healthy functioning, the emotions of the irascible appetite help to achieve that to which the pleasure appetite is directed. Emotions of the irascible appetite are, by nature, subservient to emotions of the first group. Meanwhile, in repressive neurosis, there is a pathological blockage of feelings. Some of the emotions of the irascible appetite then try to repress feelings that reflexively have been recognized as being unauthorized.

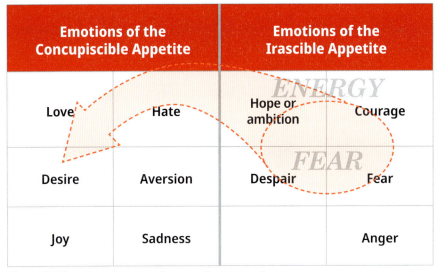

Figure 5. The phenomenon of repressive neurosis

In the neurotic reaction, a misaligned sensitive usefulness judgment (Latin: *vis cogitativa*) instinctively assesses a given emotion as inappropriate and stimulates a repressive feeling against it. The reason and the will may be fully functional, but at a given moment, their role is taken over by a sensory judgment that evokes the emotions of the irascible appetite and directs them against the experienced feeling of the pleasure appetite. In the process of repression, either the feelings of hope or ambition and courage together produce a force of emotional energy that represses some feeling of the pleasure appetite, or the feelings of despair and fear together produce a pervasive fear that similarly represses a given feeling. Hence, **two types of neurosis emerge. One is dominated by emotional energy, and the other by fear.**

In the neurotic approach to sexual desire, the reason knows that sexuality is natural and therefore good and necessary and fully legitimate; nevertheless, it is experienced as something fundamentally wrong. The sensory judgment determines its existence as negative and triggers a repressing feeling. **In neurosis, therefore, it is not rationality that proves decisive but, rather, irrational feelings.**

In neurosis, an unnecessary repressive feeling suddenly appears, stuck like a wedge between reason, will, and the repressed emotion. Consequently, the spiritual powers have no access to the repressed emotion, and so it does not attain its natural, rational expression, for it is as if buried alive. It is not annihilated, which, in any case, would be impossible; rather, it is pushed out of its natural place in the psyche and covered up by the repressing emotion. As a result, the repressed emotion is agitated like somebody trapped alive inside a coffin, eliciting outraged reactions that are completely beyond the control of reason and will.

Groundless repression of emotions gives rise to obsessive-compulsive movements that are completely beyond freedom. The person with a neurotic approach to sexuality is free, rational, and responsible in most matters, but in the sexual sphere, he or she is enslaved. This is why temptations and sexual actions arise that are completely unfree and irrational. Obsessive searches for sensations in glances, in egoistic fantasies, and in pornography increase, and outright disordered acts that cannot be tamed are committed. All kinds of perversions and serious abuses are most frequently born out of sexual neurosis.

Internal affections, when they are kept within and permitted no outlet, burn the more strongly within. This is clear in sorrow and anger which, when they are kept within, continually increase; but if they are given any kind of release outwardly, their vigor is dissipated. But a prohibition, since it threatens a penalty, compels man not to give outward expression to his desire, so that, being kept within, it burns more vigorously.

St. Thomas Aquinas

The mechanism of repressing an unwanted feeling may be shallow or deep, conscious or unconscious. It can occur only after the feeling has taken hold in the psyche or at the very beginning of its manifestation. An initially mild neurosis may, in time, increase in intensity and spread to other objects. When an unhealthy reflex of repressing a given emotion has emerged in the psyche, causing compulsive, uncontrollable reactions, this gives rise to fear and the desire to repress the threatening feeling even more strongly. A vicious circle thus comes about, with the neurosis becoming deeper and deeper. As opposed to growing in virtues, whether acquired or, even more so, those infused by grace, there is no increase in psychological freedom and ease in the good, but, on the contrary, the problem becomes more aggravated.

The sensitive usefulness judgment, which stimulates the feelings of the irascible appetite, is ordinarily under the influence of reason, but in neurosis it functions incorrectly. The root cause does not necessarily lie in the moral teaching, which may have been entirely correct. What is decisive however is the manner of its reception. The moral law, including the natural law, is rational and corresponds to human nature. Therefore, it is to be accepted and applied to life by reason. But it may happen that moral teaching is received emotionally as an irrational must or that what has been given is plainly erroneous, and in such a case, the ill-functioning sense judgment is stimulated. In neurosis, the repressive emotion is not guided by rationality. It feels the undesirable emotion in a bad way, even when reason has no doubts that this feeling is fundamentally good and fully justified.

To refuse all pleasures against reason out of dislike for them is to be dour like a boor.

St. Thomas Aquinas

To grow in chastity, one must not only understand that sexuality is natural and good but must also feel it as something good, even when disorder appears in it. It is the disorder that requires a reaction, but sexuality itself is good. It must also be remembered, of course, that conscience is an act of reason, not of emotion. In a healthy person, the feelings support the judgment of conscience, giving joy when one has done something good and releasing guilt when one has done something wrong. In a neurotic person, however, the repressive feeling precedes or even replaces the judgment of reason, causing unjustified feelings of guilt.

Neurotic repressions may concern a variety of emotions and their objects, not just sexuality. When they touch upon trivial matters, they are not dangerous and do not cause persisting disorders. If parents always react aggressively against chewing gum, their child may temporarily develop a reflex to repress the desire for chewing gum, but this will not cause any drama in the psyche. But sexuality and life's dynamic, which use the assertive emotions, are two very important spheres of life. When they are repressed, disorders are born.

Sometimes a phenomenon occurs in which it is not very clear which emotions are doing the repressing, but it is clear enough which ones are being repressed because they keep revealing themselves in a chaotic manner. A person who experiences this suffers from hysterical neurosis. In another case, it is immediately clear which emotions are doing the repressing. Then obsessive-compulsive neurosis, fear neurosis, or energy neurosis appears. In all of these neuroses, it is not the repressed feeling that should be curbed (or, to use a rather imprecise terminology, "mortified") but the repressing emotion. When the repressing fear or energy is reduced, the person returns to psychic equilibrium because, in the neurotic, the emotions are fundamentally sound but have only been misdirected.

When reading about neuroses, one should not panic and immediately talk oneself into a sickness. All people have some irregularities and rough patches in their psyches, but these sort themselves out over time, especially if a living faith is sustained. Knowledge of the functioning of the psyche and of frequently arising unhealthy mechanisms allows one to avoid erroneous paths and, what is more, facilitates the assisting of those who may have difficulties with this.

X. Fear Neurosis

Fear belongs to the set of emotions of the irascible appetite. It is a spontaneous reaction to a threat. The psychological state induced by fear causes anxiety, agitation, and sometimes a temporary paralysis and facial paleness. It prompts a swift protective response against the danger. When an unexpected car suddenly veers into one's path, the emotion of fear will prompt an immediate reaction, to get out of the way. Experiencing fear is therefore a legitimate and necessary symptom of a healthy psyche.

The problem arises, however, when the stirrings of the pleasure appetite — fascination, desire, or joy — are instinctively perceived as a threat, presumably prompting to a moral evil, and as a result, fear is immediately activated with the aim of driving the disturbing feeling out of the psyche. Such a reflex is a psychic disorder because, in a healthy person, the direction of feelings does not negate their experience. To control an exaggerated desire for pleasure, one must first recognize, or rather feel, that the desire in itself is not bad but good. It is only the irrational abandoning of oneself to excessive pleasure that needs to be restrained, not the mere feeling of desire.

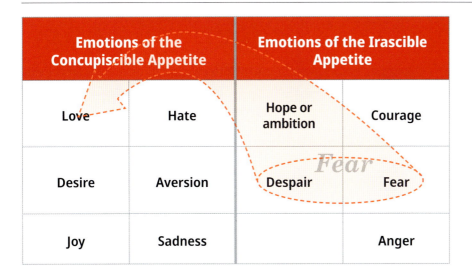

Figure 6. Fear neurosis

In fear neurosis, the emotions of fear and despair join together and turn their full force against some emotion of the pleasure appetite. Consequently, a general fear builds up in the psyche, and it tries to remove from the consciousness and feeling the undesired emotion. This is done irrationally and completely spontaneously.

When fear neurosis concerns sexuality, every experience of the sexual drive is immediately perceived as a moral evil or threat, and before reason and the will are able to react to this experience and work with it, fear forces itself in like a wedge and, with its psychic power, attempts to repress — that is, extinguish — the supposedly dangerous fire. Of course, the sexual drive cannot be eliminated from the psyche because it is part of human nature and therefore sometimes it makes itself known, but the fear neurotic defends himself against it and does so with fear. This fear is unjustified and unhealthy. Like a foreign body, it causes confusion in the psyche.

Any fear, and even more so a misdirected fear, is unsuitable for the role of the driver, yet in this neurosis it replaces reason, taking over the function of conscience. Thus, there is no peaceful integration of the sexual drive with the spiritual powers of reason and will because the emotions are stifled by a repressing fear that masquerades as the conscience. In the ensuing psychic tension, the repressed drive continues to resound, and what is more, it does so in a wild and chaotic manner. Something then pushes the neurotic person in an enslaved way toward sexual feelings and actions, and this, in turn, generates even greater fears.

The neurotic person responds to this with an even stronger repressive fear because it seems to him or her that the only defense against the threat of evil is in fear. In this vicious cycle, the fear grows and encompasses more and more issues, spinning on an endless conflict in the psyche. The person suffering from fear neurosis frequently checks whether the gas in the kitchen has been turned off because of the insecurity about himself and the constant fear. Over time, fear overcomes the entire personality, frequently reacting to purely imaginary and anticipated threats.

Fear neurosis is accompanied by chronic somatic symptoms such as insomnia, stuttering, and a stimulated imagination. Sleep is light, and dreams are colorful. In severe cases, this neurosis may lead to phobias, outbursts of anger, and then to depression and despair.

Fear neurosis is a psychic disorder caused by a misalignment of the emotions, but it is connected to or overlaps with the moral life. That which is sick seems to be confused with that which is sinful. The fear neurotic, however, is unable to differentiate these matters. Each stirring of an emotion, even an unwanted one or, rather, one that occurs prior to the discernment of conscience is already considered to be sinful. Hence, the neurotic person constantly feels guilty. The growing fear gives rise to endless scruples — that is, moral worries about minor, trivial matters (Latin: *scrupulus*, a pebble in one's shoe).

A way to achieve temporary appeasement is to confess one's faults to someone who is an authority. Scrupulous individuals, therefore, constantly go to Confession, sometimes even several times a week, to which they always bring a huge list of sins. Because they do not distinguish temptations from sins, they think that they must confess all temptations and spontaneous feelings. They fear responsibility for distant, unreal, and totally imaginary consequences of their actions. They fear that in a previous confession they did not say everything, that they did not explain all the circumstances, or that the priest did not quite hear what they said, from which they conclude that the previous confession was certainly invalid, and they want to confess everything again. They keep making impossible promises to God, which only deepens their fears and feelings of guilt.

Scrupulosity is a sickness that aggravates anxiety and fear. The scrupulous person is afraid of God; afraid of people; afraid of sins — past, future, imaginary, or doubtful; afraid of his own thoughts, imaginations, and feelings, and above all, afraid of himself. Confessing all of this provides a moment of relief, but after a few days, the fear returns. The scrupulous penitent does not seek God and His merciful grace in the sacrament but is only looking for a magical procedure that will give a moment of peace and quiet, until the fear starts to bother again. Such people are suspicious of every kindly remark, and, in fact, they do not listen to the advice given, because they are focused on something else. They are afraid that maybe they have forgotten to say something or said something inaccurately. They are concentrated on their state and not on what they might hear. Neither divine grace nor divine love nor the conscience guides them through life, but only the ever-present fear.

Fear is driven out by perfect love.

1 John 4:18

Fear neurosis is more common among women, but when a man falls into it, it is more difficult to bring him out of it.

Healing from this sickness comes about only through the reduction of fear. If any feeling in such a person is to be "mortified," it is fear. This, however, the neurotic does not want to do because it seems that fear is the only defense against potential sin. It is necessary, therefore, for the neurotic to stop considering the sensations originating from the pleasure appetite as something bad but, rather, as something normal.

Those who suffer from fear neurosis are usually intelligent, and their emotions are fundamentally sound, although they have been inappropriately blocked. It is therefore possible to explain to such a person the out-of-place mechanism repressing the feelings caused by excessive fear, and he or she will be able to understand this. Of course, merely understanding the problem does not immediately bring liberation, but it is the first step. It is important to make an act of courage so as not to be afraid of one's own feelings and sensations. This means that in the healing process, there will be a period when the repressive fear will be unblocked, and there will be a temporary feeling of defenselessness because the liberated emotions will resound while their peaceful and lasting integration has not yet taken place. One should not be alarmed by this and should move forward with confidence. In time, the hitherto repressed emotions will rightly begin to respond to the light of reason and the guidance of the will.

Open wide the doors for Christ.... Do not be afraid! Christ knows "what is in man". He alone knows it.

St. John Paul II

The person who helps the scrupulous individual to free himself or herself from fear neurosis must be characterized by kindness and understanding. In order to be able to recognize the sick neurotic deformation and then provide help, one needs to know how the emotions function in a healthy way. Supporting the suffering person in the process of liberation requires patience because arriving at psychic equilibrium takes time.

The helper does not have to be a professional therapist or a priest. An educator, a kind friend, a man or a woman, a husband or a wife can help a great deal, provided that the helper understands the essence of the spiritual and psychological life. A warm friendship combined with a basic knowledge of the human psyche is sufficient. In any case, it is better when the person suffering from fear neurosis receives clarification and guidance outside the confessional, because then the person is calmer, more inclined to a cool and rational reception of what is said, without fear.

It is important that the neurotic notices and recognizes that he or she also possesses positive qualities. Some people can detail a long list of their sins and shortcomings, but they cannot say anything positive about themselves. It will be difficult to do something good independently if one does not also believe that one has some good qualities. A kindhearted person who helps the scrupulous individual can convince him or her about this personal goodness. To love God and neighbor, we must first love ourselves — that is, see the good in ourselves. God's mercy must first be applied to ourselves, but this is easier to do when a reflection of that mercy is seen in the gestures, trust, and goodness of the person standing beside us.

Confidence ... gives great freedom and creative impetus. Freedom from idols and from fear. Creativity ... because God continually opens up paths of love to man.

Bł. Pierre Claverie, O.P.

The two best cures for neurosis are a living faith and a sense of humor about oneself. Faith means the transfer of one's difficulties onto the shoulders of the Savior, and a sense of humor allows one to let go of the serious tone and experience a little psychic ease toward oneself.

XI. Energy Neurosis

A phenomenon similar to fear neurosis is energy neurosis. The same kind of tension occurs, one caused by ill-functioning emotions. The external impression given by such a person, however, is different. The scrupulous person lives in constant anxiety and fear, and this becomes immediately apparent, while one suffering from energy neurosis gives the impression of being balanced, but in his or her attitude, there is some rigidity and inflexibility, emanating coldness.

In energy neurosis, the emotions of hope — that is, ambition and courage — combine to produce psychic energy, which, as in fear neurosis, is directed against an emotion of the pleasure appetite with the corresponding effect of removing the influence of reason and will in the respective sphere of feeling. When the psychic energy enters like a wedge that pushes away the unwanted emotion, likewise an abnormal trapping of the feeling takes place.

Emotions of the Concupiscible Appetite		Emotions of the Irascible Appetite	
Love	Hate	Hope or ambition	Fear
Desire	Aversion	Despair	Fear
Joy	Sadness		Anger

Figure 7. Energy neurosis

In principle, experiencing the energy of life is something good and does not necessarily indicate neurosis. Eagerness and courage are necessary assertive feelings that enable us to achieve what the emotions of the pleasure appetite incline us to do. In responding to challenges, it is better to engage with psychic strength than to do so sluggishly, out of a lazy obedience to necessity, or simply unwillingly. Assertive feelings add the necessary dynamism to life, and even if they are very strong in someone so that the feelings of the pleasure appetite wane, this does not mean that such a person suffers from a psychic disorder. Hardworking, enthusiastic people sometimes have weaker feelings of empathy and cordiality, so there is less warmth and sensitivity to the feelings of others in them. The strength of the emotions in each individual is slightly different, and this is quite normal.

In energy neurosis, however, the psychic force is used not to attain the object toward which the pleasure appetite inclines but to repress the emotion because it is felt to be undesirable or suspicious. When a person's upbringing has always suggested that sexual desire is something fundamentally wrong, and certainly dangerous, the resolute individual identifies every sexual sensation as something that must be interiorly repressed and does so with emotional force.

The repression of the sexual drive with energy does not lead to psychic freedom. This repression gives the appearance of efficiency, self-confidence, and strict control, but over time, all spontaneity fades in such people and is replaced by a consciously programmed mask. These people lose interest, and there are few things that can arouse their spontaneous fascination.

Those suffering from energy neurosis are unnaturally tense, incapable of emotional contact. Their reactions become dry and rigid. They are lonely, but often they are unaware of their loneliness because they have become accustomed to it. They are emotionally self-sufficient, and this is because there is a sort of cold gap between them and others. When somebody directs affection toward them, they feel as if they are encountering a wall.

Contrary to fear neurotics, these individuals are so in control of themselves that they keep their imaginations in check. They do not dream much, and they sleep deeply to make up for the psychic fatigue resulting from constant forceful repression. Thus, they often feel exhausted, and the ongoing tension occasionally erupts in aggression.

The repression of an unwanted emotion by energy prevents its virtuous integration. The emotion stuffed into the psyche occasionally rebels, but it does so in a wild, enslaved manner. Thus, in such a neurotic, obsessive-compulsive symptoms appear that are outside the sphere of freedom. When the sexual drive is repressed with energy, there are moments when the person feels that something is pushing to look for pornography, to be obsessed with sex, to accumulate sensations all the time, and it is not possible to tame this.

Thus, under the mask of a well-balanced, self-confident personality hide uncontrollable outbursts of repressed feelings generating deep shame and anxiety. The immediate reaction to this is to mobilize psychic energy — that is, to take control of the situation — but here, too, a vicious cycle takes place. Instead of virtue growing so that the appropriate good could be easily, quickly, and pleasantly attained, the loop deepens and the falls become more frequent and more disturbing. Against this background, perverse abuses are born.

As in the case of fear neurosis, the sphere of sick feelings and their moral evaluation overlap. The energy neurotic very much desires honesty, but in his moral horizon, the first to emerge are moral obligation and a firm purpose of amendment. The attempt to enforce change, however, is not an act of the will, a spiritual power that is attracted by the good, and still less a work of charity; rather, it is an act of repressing emotions, those of hope and ambition and courage, which together produce the repressing psychic energy. There is thus a confusion of the will with the emotions of the irascible appetite. The will is spiritual, and the emotions are corporeal, manifested in a clenched fist or a grimace.

I picture a father who has two children, mischievous and disobedient, and when he comes to punish them, he sees one of them who trembles and gets away from him in terror, having, however, in the bottom of his heart the feeling that he deserves to be punished; and his brother, on the contrary, throws himself into his father's arms ... and asks his father to punish *him with a* kiss. *I do not believe that the heart of a happy father could resist the filial confidence of his child.... He realizes, however, that more than once his son will fall into the same faults, but he is prepared to pardon him always, if his son takes him by his heart.*

St. Thérèse of Lisieux

Energy neurosis is the psychic, emotional equivalent of the heresy of Pelagianism. Its essence is the negation of grace. Instead of inviting God's power into one's psyche in faith and charity, such a neurotic counts on his own self-sufficiency. He does not know that steps of improvement are possible only if, in humility, he gives God His place.

This, however, the energy neurotic does not do — because he thinks that everything depends on his own power. He thinks that he cannot approach

God with his sins, as if moral perfection were a necessary prerequisite for any contact with God! Thus, there is no place here for a childlike, trusting relationship with God, and only a reliance on moral rectitude, which is to be achieved on one's own.

This is why we are bold enough to approach God in complete confidence, through our faith in him.

Ephesians 3:12

Pelagianism leads to terrible rigor, first toward ourselves and then toward others. When moral perfection and full emotional control are assumed to be achievable on one's own, by force, without the help of grace, any failure to attain them is interpreted as a serious moral fault. Rigid, blocked educators then demand the same in others.

These neurotics are also intelligent, and the false mechanism of their disorder can be explained to them. In order for healing to take place, it is necessary that the repressive energy be reduced. This means abandoning the previous way of defending oneself against a moral threat and recognizing that a repressed feeling has the right to emerge and move in the psyche. In the process of release, the energy neurotic may now want to stimulate the repressed feeling or forcefully repress the unnecessary energy. This is not to be done. Once a feeling is no longer repressed, it will come to life on its own, and after a brief period of disquiet, it will find the right expression.

An energy neurotic can be advised to develop those interests that still fascinate him and to which he can devote himself gratuitously, for sheer pleasure. Feelings should not be artificially stimulated because the emotional life, by its very nature, is passive. It allows itself to be carried away and this is proper and normal. The change from the dominance of efficiency to the joyful appreciation of affectivity comes about not immediately but gradually, and therefore time is needed.

I shall cleanse you of all your defilement.... I shall give you a new heart, and put a new spirit in you; I shall remove the heart of stone from your bodies and give you a heart of flesh instead.

Ezekiel 36:25–26

Often it turns out that a correction in the understanding of Christian morality is needed. A childlike friendly relationship with God is more important than the execution of cold obligation. It is the theological virtues and not the moral virtues that are to have the primary and leading role. The moral law is an expression of God's wisdom that guides us to happiness and not of the offended and arbitrary will of a powerful tyrant. It is addressed to human reason and not to emotional compulsion. Moreover, the summit of God's law is the new law of grace, the law of the gospel, whose essential power is the Holy Spirit Himself, dwelling in the soul.

XII. Why Is This So Difficult?

Feelings thrill us, draw us into the unknown, involving not only the soul but also the body — that is, laughter, tears, anger, excitement, disgust, sexual desire, sadness, and in all of this lie their beauty and charm. And so it is meant to be, because that is their quality. Thanks to them, we know and feel that we are truly alive.

Sometimes, however, feelings carry us too far — forcibly, as it were — and then anxiety and shame come about, and misunderstandings erupt between people. Emotions are a testimony not only to corporeality but also to chaos, which we are not always capable of dealing with. In the case of more serious dysfunctions, distorted tendencies, addictions, and abuse result from emotional disorder.

Why, despite good intentions and religious practices, does not everything go smoothly with the emotions? Instead of having an integration of the emotional sphere with the spiritual as well as with charity infused in the soul by God, sometimes one attempts to control himself forcibly through the will, or even worse, has neurotic reactions with an exaggerated, misplaced fear or energy. Why does this happen, even though it does not grant inner peace?

Can ingrained habits in the treatment of one's emotions be undone? If so, how? Many addicts would love to break free, but despite prayers and efforts, the difficulty remains and causes serious confusion in life. Why?

Emotions are awakened by stimuli that strike through the cognitive senses. Among them are memory, which stores experience and knowledge, and also the sensitive usefulness judgment (Latin: *vis cogitativa*). This judgment instinctively evaluates sensations and images evoked by the imagination and then provokes an emotional response.

The sensitive usefulness judgment does not function in us as it does in wild animals. In those animals, nature leads directly to what is appropriate and, through their animal usefulness judgment (Latin: *vis aestimativa*), protects them from danger. When a human trains an animal, permanently shaping its sensory judgment, the animal acts in a way that is unusual for a wild creature. Similarly, and even more so, in the human sensitive usefulness judgment, since it is susceptible to the influence of reason and a broader social experience, instinctive habits can be formed, provoking specific associations. Thus, for example, we learn languages and acquire manual and artistic skills.

It happens in people that this automatic sensory judgment reflex has been misguided, contrary to the nature of things, and over a long period of time. This is not necessarily the result of conscious training, but something similar may occur as a result of past experiences, habit, the influence of the environment, or repeated sins and, ultimately, as a consequence of Original Sin. Thus, a skewed sensitive usefulness judgment, being a part of the psyche, resonates and connects with reason, prompting a specific, not necessarily appropriate action. And hence it influences actions.

If a mother, out of care for her child's health, adds raspberry juice to an unsavory medicine in order to sweeten it, then a reflex of distaste may be created in the child's psyche toward that juice. Years later, of course, reason will understand what it was all about, but raspberry juice may still bear an unpleasant association. This is so because a directed usefulness judgment generates a negative assessment, which is sensory and not rational.

In someone who has an alcoholic father, the memory of family quarrels might be so unpleasant that an aversion to liquor develops. As an adult, the person avoids liquor and manages to live this way until, suddenly, difficult unforeseen stresses arise, and then, as if unknowingly, he reaches for the bottle. He knows rationally that this is not right, but he does so because the entrenched sensitive usefulness judgment prompts him to seek solace in alcohol.

The more potent the soothing agent, the more difficult it is to break free from it. When sadness is mitigated with stimulants or drugs that leave permanent traces in the brain, the directed usefulness judgment continues to suggest them. The sadness may be legitimate, resulting from a genuinely distressing situation, but the manner of dealing with it is inappropriate. Nevertheless, this solution is tempting, because the psyche has already been grounded in this way.

Something similar happens in the sexual sphere. Incorrect associations regarding sexuality can be a result of an insecure or erroneous upbringing, and even more so, they may derive from abuse that someone has experienced or pornography that someone has watched.

In all of these examples, the sensitive usefulness judgment instinctively pronounces an incorrect assessment that is contrary to human nature and its basic finality, but this reflex is perceived as one's own, and therefore it seems natural. This provokes an emotional reaction, but since it is contrary to nature, it generates confusion instead of inclining to virtue. Anxiety then pleads for a forceful or neurotic defense, and the psyche is internally entangled.

Sometimes there emerge **instinctive inclinations that are unnatural**, contrary to human nature and its finality. Something then pushes toward emotional reactions that are irrational, unnatural. Following them does not give inner peace, and combating them seems impossible.

Thus something which is "against human nature" (contra naturam), either as regards reason or as regards physical preservation, may happen to be in harmony with the natural needs (connaturale) of this man because in him nature is ailing.... Some men by habituation come to take pleasure in cannibalism, or in copulation with beasts or with their own sex, or in other things not in accord with human nature.

St. Thomas Aquinas

Some accept their disordered tendencies, telling themselves that this is how they are and always will be, while others try to struggle against them, but often they do so by force, which eventually proves ineffective and tiresome. An easy response to this is aggression, toward oneself or others, or depression, or flooding the problem with an artificial soothing agent that eventually becomes addictive. Either way, it often ends in mental and moral degeneration.

So what is the way out of this?

There are two aspects to note — one natural and the other supernatural.

A poorly functioning sensitive usefulness judgment has to be corrected. This is not simple or easy. First, thinking about the matter must be corrected. Humanity, its nature and meaning, must be understood. When, however, there are erroneous theories or total confusion and chaos in the mind, it is hardly surprising that reason, when it works practically, cannot distance itself from sensory reflexes.

Correcting theoretical thinking is easier than straightening out sensory reflexes, but the latter will not begin at all if the mind persists in error. Ensuring a correct understanding of human nature, the psyche, and the finality of the faculties in itself will not automatically translate into a correct perception of the sensory judgment. But at least it is the first step toward healing.

For example, someone may have an instinctive dislike of people in authority. He was brought up by a single mother, and his father appeared only sporadically and caused rows. And so a spontaneous reaction of aggression was generated, not only toward the father but toward all those who have any authority. Reason will suggest that resistance and resentment toward the boss at work is irrational, but the emotions will fume, provoking unjustified anger. Liberation from this unhealthy emotional reaction will not be possible if such a person adopts anarchist views and rebels against all authority on principle.

The rectitude of the appetitive faculty in regard to the end is the measure of truth for the practical reason.

St. Thomas Aquinas

Since the usefulness judgment is sensual, a healing psychotherapy may be applied at this point. Its domain is that dimension of the psyche that has its basis in the body. However, it must understand the sense and finality of the psychic powers, and so psychotherapy needs a deeper philosophical view in which empirical observations are situated.

Untangling bad habits accrued in the sensitive usefulness judgment can be done only if one knows what is really good, in accordance with the truth and the innate finality of the psyche. When the therapist does not know this, because he is stuck in intellectual skepticism and therefore in a relativistic vacuum, he will be of little help.

Furthermore, the spiritual life, and therefore the life of grace, should not be replaced by psychotherapy. A precise distinction must be made between the spheres of operation. Otherwise, a kind of substitute religion will be produced.

The more aged the distortion of sensory judgment, the slower the healing will be. When judgment tends in the opposite direction to the essential finality of nature, the integration of the emotions with the spiritual powers is hindered. Then the virtues, both those acquired naturally and those infused by grace, do not manifest themselves easily, quickly, with pleasure, and creatively. On the contrary, a seed of disorder persists in the psyche and complicates life.

The great saints knew about this. Everyone carries some wounds in the psyche or soul because we are all children of Adam. And therefore, we all need the grace of God.

Out of the depths I cry unto thee, O Lord.

Ps. 130:1

I can see that my body follows a different law that battles against the law which my reason dictates. This is what makes me a prisoner.... Who will rescue me from this body doomed to death? Thanks be to God through Jesus Christ our Lord!"

Romans 7:23–25

He who believes in Christ can count on the power that flows from His cross. This is what spiritual childhood is all about. Since the Lord has freely and completely unveiled His love, which has the power to heal, there is no need to panic and to concentrate on our weaknesses. With confidence, like a child, we can count on God's help, and we can maintain a distance toward ourselves and a sense of humor.

Coming to terms with oneself and growing in virtue will not come about without struggle, but in the end, it is not just a battle against resurgent degenerate tendencies but a struggle to ensure that God will have priority, that faith will go so far as to believe that grace can penetrate the deepest recesses of the psyche and the soul. Precisely where there is the greatest poverty, there we can rely on God with childlike sincerity and trust. This is why we must resolutely maintain a lively faith and charity directed toward God — that is, the primacy of the theological virtues, which are more important than the moral virtues.

What is soilèd, make Thou pure;
What is wounded, work its cure;
What is parchèd, fructify;
What is rigid, gently bend;
What is frozen, warmly tend;
Strengthen what goes erringly.

Cardinal Stephen Langton

All the evils experienced in life, be they physical, moral, external, or psychological, can ultimately serve the glory of God. They must be used as a springboard to land ever deeper and more frequently in the arms of God Himself.

XIII. Sexual Emotions

There is no doubt that sexuality, with all its bodily, physiological, emotional, and even spiritual baggage, serves the transmission of life. For humans, new life requires long-term support, care, and nurturing, and for this reason, sexuality binds couples together and induces them to give their interpersonal bond a lasting, familial, self-sacrificing character. The sexual drive is astonishingly powerful because it is crucial for the survival of the human species.

Furthermore, the marital bond is a singular place where the love that comes from God Himself may manifest itself when it is invoked by faith. All desire their sexuality to be a vehicle of supreme love, including those who distort sexuality because they cannot cope with it. Even a tainted sexuality says something, if only erroneously, about love and about what goes on in the heart.

Since the sexual drive has such an important purpose, the twisting of its meaning and its repression generate psychological and moral difficulties. The denial of other, less significant inclinations and desires — for example, musical talent — does not necessarily cause neurosis. In contrast, the repression of sexuality always leads to emotional perturbation.

The answer to these disturbances is not to let the sexual drive loose, giving it free rein. Driving a fast vehicle without any brakes always ends badly, for the driver and often for others.

Sexual feelings are good and strong, but all must wrestle with them and learn how to integrate their dynamics within responsible choices and within life. The question is whether one will try to do this in a neurotic way, or by sheer force of will, or whether, by faith, one will allow God's power into the psyche, so that chastity, received with grace and then consciously cultivated, will keep the impetuosity of the drive in such a way that it may be given to the loved one with whom one goes through life.

The integration of emotionality is difficult when the instinctive reflex, generated by the sensitive usefulness judgment, turns out to be at odds with the natural end of things. This judgment links with the judgment of reason and directly prompts actions. In the heat of action, there is no time for theoretical moral agonizing. Steps are undertaken with haste. Of course, conscience — that is, reason — may consider the matter both before and after the act, but in most reactions and practical movements, everything happens in an instant. So it is worth noting the meaning that is instinctively given to sexuality by virtue of the sensory judgment. Has it not been distorted by habits and external influences?

When sexuality resounds in the psyche and in the body, it releases a pleasurable sensation. In men, the purely physical sensation is dominant. Women are more sensitive to emotional excitement. The fact that sexuality is pleasurable is by nature good. It happens, however, that as soon as it speaks up, a reflex is immediately activated that suggests that "sex has to be safe," and often, more than the possibility of contracting an infectious disease, one thinks of the child who may be conceived, who may show his innocent helplessness and claim his rights. So the child, who is not yet there and who may never exist at all, is already branded in the psyche as a threatening enemy.

Meanwhile, true love, one that unites not only bodies but, above all, persons, is not afraid of fragility and dependence. Lovers reveal to one another the childlike dimension of their souls, that in some issue they are helpless and in need, and also that they may respond to the other's need. Recognizing the childlike fragility of one's psyche and that of the other, and the mutual revealing of this to one another, generates a readiness to care and protect. It is no wonder, then, that in time, true love expands the heart and produces a willingness to accept the infant who, dependent, innocent, and uncomplicated, waits in trust for responsible, caring parental love.

But when this willingness is lacking in the spiritual life and, in the place of caring, an instinctive reflex of aversion or even hostility toward the child appears, the integration of sexuality proves to be difficult. In order for a person to direct the sexual sphere, he or she must treat it, in accordance with its natural end, as something that is intrinsically good and not evil. When sexuality is associated in a negative way, as a threat, then the slipping into neurotic repression or an attempt to control it uniquely by willpower easily becomes automatic. Chastity, which enables the integration and wise directing of the sexual drive — whether it is natural and acquired with difficulty or is the fruit of grace summoned by faith — needs at its base a correct and positive interpretation of the meaning of sexuality, one not in conflict with the nature of things.

What is one to do, then, when instinctively the sexual drive is associated only recreationally, with the exclusion of the prospect of parenthood? Pornography, as well as the sexuality present in advertising, films, and seductive gestures, suggest a purely consumerist approach to sexual stimuli, providing immediate sensations. In this gathering of gratification, egoism is dominant. In men, the desire for bodily sensations plays a greater role; selfishness occurs also in women, although, since they are more emotional, their reactions may appear "purer." Feeding on shallow romances and movies that promote not values but only the maximization of emotional, titillating, empty sensations is also egoistic, and therefore it is a kind of "emotional pornography."

It is necessary that each and every conjugal act is located within its intrinsic purpose of procreating human life. This doctrine ... is based on the indissoluble connection ... which couples may not on their own initiative break between the unitive significance and the procreative significance that both pertain to the conjugal act. Moreover due to the inherent nature of the connection of these significances, the conjugal act, while uniting husband and wife in the deepest tie, also renders them apt to generate new life in accord with the laws that are written into the very nature of man and woman. And if each of these essential qualities, the unitive and the procreative, is preserved, the use of marriage fully retains its sense of true mutual love and its ordination to the supreme responsibility of parenthood to which man is called.

St. Paul VI

When personal, not necessarily culpable experiences have generated an incorrect reading of the sexual drive in the sensory impulse, one that is hostile toward marriage and the transmission of life, its integration into mature, wise, and free moves will be difficult. A theoretical understanding of the meaning of sexuality is a good starting point, but, in itself, it is insufficient. What is also needed is a correction of the instinctive associations so that a full appreciation of sexuality and its basic natural end may occur. This comes about slowly, as a result of patient struggle with oneself and a correct way of thinking.

Sexual sensitivity brings people together and makes them love one another. The otherness of the opposite sex intrigues and attracts. God created woman so that she would break the spiritual loneliness of the male and, with her person, faith, and capacity for selfless giving, show him how close is God and how tender is His love, which need not be feared. A woman is happiest when a man begins to sense the goodness of God as she perceives it, and he takes this spiritual experience of hers into himself and allows it to transform him. The man, on the other hand is happy when, with his responsible caring gift, he protects, serves, and guides his wife and children.

It is not good that the man should be alone.

Genesis 2:18

He took his wife to his home.

Matthew 1:24

When sexual contact between a man and a woman confirms the mutual awareness that, with their whole selves, they are walking through life together toward eternity and are helping one another on this path, it also then expresses true love, without egoism.

Sexuality calls for the transmission of life. It can be reciprocally accepted and mutually offered without falsehood when there is an acceptance of the goodness of life and a willingness to transmit it precisely through the person of the spouse, in appreciation of the parental abilities that they both have.

Husbands may therefore ask themselves: **Is my wife becoming a better, more valuable person under my influence? Am I becoming a better, more generous person under her influence? Do I want to have a daughter like her? Am I happy that it is precisely my wife, with her charm and life wisdom, who is the mother of our children? Am I content with the children (and grandchildren) that we have?**

And wives may ask themselves: **Is my husband becoming someone better, more reliable under my influence? Am I becoming more honest by peeking into his world of values? Do I want to have a son like him? Am I overjoyed that it is precisely my husband, with his thinking and principles, who is the father of our children? Am I content with the children (and grandchildren) that we have?**

When sexual experiences are devoid of appreciation for the shared path of life and parenthood, they are isolated. Then there is an exclusive focus on gratification, which turns sex into a kind of drug or idol. This breeds and deepens egoism. And when it happens that the provision of sexual experiences at a given time is impossible, tiring, or unwanted, aggression often ensues. Manipulation and serious abuses result from this. Sex then ceases to be a privileged place to experience love. The degeneration of homeless men banished to the streets by their wives stems most often from this.

When one notices that the reflexive sensitive judgment concerning sexuality is incorrect, one should not immediately panic because then a neurotic entanglement may easily come about. In reaching maturity, the psyche has to be put in order, but this is done slowly. Similarly, the fact that young boys are fascinated by an older friend and girls prefer their own company should not be interpreted as meaning that a disorder has developed. This is normal. Besides, there is no such thing as "homosexual orientation." There are homosexual inclinations — shallow, deeper, temporary, or longer-lasting — but one should not conclude from this that there is a permanent condition that defines a person's identity.

Everyone needs to domesticate their sexual dynamics through the virtue of chastity. In marriage, too, one must know how to manage the drive so that it does not enslave or distort life. Nurturing a living faith that sustains grace in the psyche is a great benefit because it helps to avoid taking "shortcuts" through forceful or neurotic solutions.

It is obvious that those who have made a vow of lifelong celibacy or virginity to God likewise need to take a healthy approach to their sexuality. They, too, are prone to an erroneous reflex evaluation of sex and need to correct it in themselves. In order to make a gift to God of one's sexual drive, it has to be instinctively recognized as something good. We do not give bad things to God! It should come as no surprise that clergy often have difficulty with this. They, too, are marked by the sins of our time, but they can offer this weakness to God in childlike trust. Do they do so? That depends on whether their thinking is correct and whether they really are going through a spiritual combat and struggling to ensure a place for God in their psyches and souls, or whether maybe they have given up. Above all, it depends on whether they are really praying.

XIV. Assertive Emotions

Both humans and animals have the emotions of hope or ambition, courage, and anger. Each of these provides strength, thanks to which we have the drive needed to undertake difficult tasks. Anger is necessary because sometimes we have to be outraged at a given situation in order to start changing it.

We all possess these emotions, even though their dynamics vary. With their bodily power, they support the spiritual will. Free choice discerns the object, which attracts by its very truth and goodness, while the assertive feelings assist, but sometimes also hinder, when they precede the cool rationality and deliberate willing. The impulsiveness of feelings does not deprive them of their natural dignity, and they are always necessary, but they must be guided so as to be in accord with the truth.

When this focus is lacking, assertive feelings can easily turn into aggression.

It is a bad sign when someone seeks to boost himself and others by harboring mendacious anger and suspicion and hurling trumped-up accusations at his opponent. Temporarily this may give the person the strength to act, but in reality it is only a despicable cover-up that conceals inner weakness and a lack of arguments.

Problems also arise when, under the influence of a faulty upbringing or an unhealthy environment, one falls into the other extreme of thinking that having a passion for life is to be avoided. This leads to the repression of assertive emotions. Since those feelings are important and necessary, their denial, as in the case of repression of the sexual drive, leads to neurosis.

The repression of initiative, whether through mismanaged fear or through life energy directed against itself, is a serious disorder. People who were told that they should not speak up and that they have no right to take independent steps, as somebody else will think and decide for them, or that they must never under any circumstances experience anger, are internally broken.

Such people are incapable of living on their own account. They are excessively passive, apathetic, and unable to react to that which is wrong around them. Sometimes they perceive dishonesty and falsehood and assess them rationally, but they remain silent because they are incapable of becoming angry. And so bad situations go on for years without any resistance because those who could have responded to them do not have the strength to take a stand. They prefer to withdraw because instinctively they judge that this is the right thing to do.

Such a false, deeply wounding psychological mechanism, which is essentially neurotic, prevails in societies that are devoid of personalism and therefore also of democracy. When everyone is afraid and thinks that it is better to lie low, better not to stick one's neck out, the country is stuck in stagnation. People live by the Russian proverb: "Beat with your forehead lower: the sky is too high, and the face of the earth is nearer." Then those who, with their initiatives, could have contributed to the social, political, and economic world prefer to back out and go through life unnoticed. Their subservience or even servility toward those in power is a mask that conceals their immaturity and a wasted life.

Long-term totalitarian rule made possible by the passivity of society causes serious injury. When a man is unable to take responsibility for himself and his family, when he returns from work dissatisfied or even disgusted by what he sees there, he feels psychologically paralyzed and is unhappy. Social stagnation, degeneration of life, and the alcoholism of broken people are direct consequences of the repression of assertive feelings.

Totalitarianism creates an unusually subtle system for achieving the seduction, corruption, and, ultimately, the self-destruction of the personality. The final product is a person who has so lost track of himself, and has squandered his abilities and attachments to such an extent that he gains pleasure from the fact that he is scum.
Vladimir D. Topolianskij

When such an environment prevails, there is no creative, prudent, organic social work undertaken for the good of others, and only violent and tragic revolutionary outbursts occur, after which apathy and discouragement return.

This neurosis is not only the fruit of brutal dictatorships. It also appears with improper models of cultural and family life. There are men who never acquire autonomous maturity because they are constantly dependent on their overprotective mothers. Their mothers do not want to concede that their sons have lives of their own. These men constantly have to fill their mothers' spiritual and moral void, and so they are permanently infantile.

Such models of life destroy families. A successful marriage consists of two columns, standing firmly and independently, joined by an arch. When one column is weak and leans on the other or, worse still, on somebody else, the marriage is flawed. A wife is not meant to be a mother to her immature husband, nor is the mother-in-law meant to be a support to either of them. There are marriages that claim to be conflict-free, but this is because one party has given up on everything. Each of them has to take care of his or her own maturity because only then can they contribute something personal to the other and to their lives.

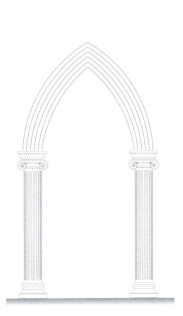

Figure 8. A successful marriage: two columns joined with an arch

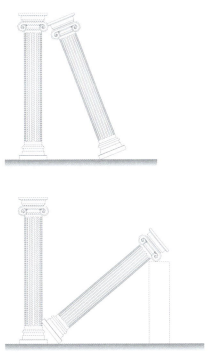

Figure 9. A flawed marriage: one column leaning on someone else

Where there is a permanent resignation to the fact that others limit and manipulate the personality, regardless of whether this occurs in the wider society, in the workplace, in a religious community, or in a narrow family circle, it is unbearable. In the same way as with the repression of sexual feelings, the blocking of assertive feelings causes irrational outbursts of aggression and periods of depression. Hence the easy escape to some lesser or greater drug.

A living faith, which invokes grace, helps in dealing with ourselves, but we must beware of false associations. We must be like children before God and cultivate a trusting reliance on Him, even and especially when the memory of sins troubles us, whereas in the face of life and its challenges, we have to be grown-ups, taking up challenges competently and with responsibility.

These orders should not be reversed, mistakenly believing that one must be strong toward God and infantile in life!

There is nothing I cannot master with the help of the One who gives me strength.

Philippians 4:13

Assertive feelings are the fabric of hope — not the theological hope that refers to God but the hope that has to do with current affairs, traditionally termed "magnanimity." It gives the strength and courage to act. Humility recognizes the primacy of God, but it should not be confused with the vice of pusillanimity (small-mindedness), which discourages responsibility.

Likewise, one should not exaggerate in the other direction, setting one's own plans against God or imposing one's own ideas on Him. Such ideological manipulation of God, demanding that He implement our agenda, destroys childlike trust and openness to God's mysterious hand that guides through life.

Well-functioning assertive feelings give enthusiasm to work, bring order to the psyche, and strengthen psychic resilience. This concept of resilience, taken from physics, suggests the internal strength of metal rods. A struck rod bends but then straightens out on its own. Psychic resilience denotes, therefore, the ability to withstand blows without panic or emotional breakdown.

Let your Spirit descend and renew the face of the earth … of this land.

St. John Paul II

XV. Happiness

Emotional experiences should not be equated with happiness. Feelings are corporeal, and therefore, they are close, immediate; when we experience them, we instantly recognize that something is going on. Happiness is deeper, although joy and pleasure are indicators suggesting where authentic goodness lies.

Emotions are empty when they do not express anything important. Shallow advertising, horror movies, the proliferation of sensual pleasures and pornography stimulate but are ultimately exhausting. Sterile emotional gratification rushes the adrenaline, but so what? Similarly, when one observes public or political affairs and sees only emotion, it means that one understands nothing.

The same has to be said of religious experiences. They should not be stimulated by a clenching of the fist or a contortion of the face, forcing oneself to "feel" something during prayer. And one should not blame oneself when religious feelings are weak or do not appear at all.

Feelings, by their very nature, respond to stimuli, and when they are linked to values recognized by reason, they add flavor to life. Spontaneous delight in true goodness or sadness at one's own or another's suffering is an expression of authenticity and humanity.

But happiness is deeper than emotional sensations. It results from the pursuit of that which is real, important, and good, which fully corresponds to human nature, both in its physical and spiritual dimensions, even if this requires effort.

Happiness is defined as the gradual transfer towards difficulties of an increasingly higher order.

Feliks Koneczny

A person working at a machine concentrates on the work in progress and does not think about the heat that the machine gives off. Similarly, a person passionately committed to a good cause pursues his goal and does not think about happiness but experiences it.

Happiness ought not to be sought, for it comes by itself when one's attention is directed toward something that is truly good, and thus when one reaches beyond oneself, beyond one's own states and feelings. Ultimately, reason tends toward the highest truth, and the will allows itself to be drawn by the highest good.

There is more happiness in giving than in receiving.

Acts 20:35

Sorting out tangled-up feelings cannot be the primary goal of life. Neither should concern for the flourishing of one's personality be at the center of attention. Whoever seeks for happiness or personal development is not aiming at something outside of him but is always concerned with his own self. He goes in circles around himself and soon becomes bored.

Communing with God, Who first, uninvited, stood in our way, attracted us, and encouraged us to love, liberates us from the prison of our own psyches. When we take care that loving God in everything and in others for His sake becomes fundamental, then happiness comes about, and it is so profound that it is described as a "blessing" or "beatitude." Then there is an incidental internal ordering of the psyche, and we flourish. But all this happens according to God's plan and timing, not ours.

In the depths of our being there is a certain sense of happiness that is identified with our sense of the true goodness. This comes from God and draws us to Him. It is imperative for us to rediscover this. It is this desire which awakens in us the message of the Gospel Beatitudes and makes them resound within us.... The predominant mentality of our times has moved the center of gravity in morality from the consideration of happiness to the concern for duty, respect for obligations and legal imperatives. We need a veritable intellectual conversion in order to give to delectation and happiness the role that they had in a virtue ethics of which Saint Thomas is the most systematic interpreter.
Fr. Servais Pinckaers, O.P.

Traditionally, it is said that the fruits of charity are joy and peace. This joy is spiritual, stemming from a relationship with God, and it is deeper than emotional joy, although it does echo within it.

Peace does not mean tranquility, where nothing happens, as in a graveyard. Peace appears in the community when everyone knows his or her place and duties and performs them with self-sacrifice. Similarly, in the psyche, peace comes about when all the powers perform their functions. No emotion, no part of the psyche, is repressed, and everything moves toward the proper ends.

We have to maintain spiritual joy within ourselves. It is not a case of either having it or not having it. We have to rejoice in God, especially when we perceive His presence in the beauty of people and nature and, even more so, in His accompanying care, power, and forgiveness. During the liturgy, religious enthusiasm should not be aroused artificially, but neither should we behave like a silent bore who does not speak at a party and infects everybody with his dullness. Liturgy is an opportunity to express faith and love internally, believing that activated faith touches God.

Spiritual joy is, above all, in the reason and in the will, which are directed toward God through faith and charity, and any echo of this in religious feelings is secondary.

The desert fathers warned against a paralyzing sadness called acedia. It is a sadness toward God, stemming from the awareness that He simply is and calls toward Himself. This difficulty often blocks men. They close themselves off and flee from God, preferring constant distractions. They then make an idol of their work or get bogged down in being occupied with self, being indifferent to others, if only to free themselves from the terrifying prospect of encountering God.

The demon of acedia, called the demon of the midday is the most serious.... At first it gives the impression that the sun is moving slowly or perhaps it is at a standstill and the day consists of fifty hours. Then it forces constant gazing out the window and going outside in order to check the time. It directs the gaze in all directions, hoping that somebody will come. In addition, it causes resentment about where one is, one's way of living and working. It suggests that there is no love among people and no one will bring comfort anymore.

St. Evagrius of Pontus

Spending time with God comes easier for women. Women can sing to Him in the chapel, and this does not bring them sadness. But since they are not indifferent to people, they perceive the trifles and achievements of others, and this sometimes gives rise to envy — that is, sadness at somebody else's success.

When sadness caused by the disturbing proximity of God or the success of others takes possession of the soul, it is easy to wallow in bitterness and resentment. The pain of the psyche then renews itself, stimulating the imagination, and gives no peace. Redirecting this pain toward faith in God and toward charity, which is concern for the sanctity of the other, immediately liberates the troubled psyche.

It is a good practice to find pleasure in silence, which is full of God. Shallow people cannot stand silence. They constantly have to talk, have to wear headphones and listen to music — not necessarily soothing but providing noise. This is because they hate situations that remind them of the chaos that is within them.

Everyone needs a bit of a desert in which, lying on an open expanse of sand, one perceives the vastness of the heavens. It is necessary to have space and time for rest, with time wisely set aside to rejuvenate strength. Then, in the soul, the head, and the psyche, matters sort themselves out according to the hierarchy of importance, and appropriate conclusions are drawn.

When the fundamental axis toward God is sustained and deepened, all inclinations, interests, passions, and preoccupations, and therefore also feelings, find their proper place without stifling, without repression, without the amputation of anything. One then discovers that the virtues do not tire because they express a joyful, creative generosity.

The affections require something more vast and more enduring than anything created.... The contemplation of Him, and nothing but it, is able fully to open and relieve the mind, to unlock, occupy, and fix our affections.

St. John Henry Newman

One last remark: It is important to have a sense of humor—that is, the ability to see an amusing element in everything. This is a sign of inner freedom, which provides a healthy balance in life.

XVI. Atonement

The word "atonement" appears in English-language theology, as well as in literature, in poetry, and even in film titles. In the Polish language, there is no equivalent of this word, and therefore it is difficult to grasp its reality. Following the structure of the word and its rare, somewhat artificial Latin root (*adunamentum*), it should be translated as "unification," or even "working toward union," but not "reconciliation," because in Polish it denotes a horizontal process of agreement between conflicting parties.

Meanwhile, "atonement" speaks of the objective, as it were, vertical work of Jesus accomplished on the Cross and in the Resurrection. The fruits of this are available through faith and in the sacraments. This can be approximated by the word "expiation" or the biblical term "redemption" (1 Pet. 1:18–19), but if it were a ransom, the question immediately arises as to who traded with whom, who was paid, and why? Did Jesus have to suffer for our sins? What is the connection between our moral and mental disorder and this death?

The Church has always believed that the death and Resurrection of Jesus are fundamental to our liberation from sin, but explaining this did not come easily. In antiquity, various colorful but unsatisfactory metaphors were devised. Origen wrote that Jesus traded His soul to the devil, thus buying our liberation. St. Gregory of Nyssa spoke of the bait of the fisherman: The divinity of Jesus hid itself in His humanity, and in Jesus' death on the Cross the devil swallowed the bait along with the hook. St Augustine compared Jesus' death to a mousetrap: The devil sniffed out Jesus' blood, approached, and was caught himself.

These images capture something, but they also give rise to strange associations. They suggest that the devil has some kind of due with which, supposedly, God must reckon. This is not the case. The evil spirit does have power over sinners, but this is not some natural right of his; rather, it was given to him by God. Furthermore, if this was a trade, it would mean that Jesus offered Himself to the devil. That is impossible. The Mass is a bloodless repetition of this sacrifice but not offered to the devil!

So it was not a question of some special entitlement of the devil that, in justice, had to be respected. Nor can it be said that Jesus played unfairly with the devil, for Jesus does not deceive anyone.

Another interpretation, sometimes appearing in religious chants, says that this sacrifice was to appease the wrath of the heavenly Father. This, too, is wrong. What kind of Father would demand the cruel death of His Son as the price of our salvation?

It was not until St. Thomas Aquinas that a balanced interpretation was proposed. Every sin is contrary to the purpose of human nature and its powers. It, therefore, causes a disorder in the psyche, which hurts. We would like to free ourselves from it, but we are unable to do so, and what is worse, every sin encourages further sin. And so, the sinner finds himself in a trap. God, however, does not react to this with immediate thunderbolts but patiently waits until the effects of sin themselves show that something has gone wrong. This strengthens the natural sense of justice, the discernment of true goodness, and the conviction that one should not declare oneself in favor of evil.

The devil may be compared here to an executioner who acts by virtue of a committed authority. His torment confirms the abnormality of the situation and makes one aware of hitherto hidden, unnoticed sins. The devilish confusion, permitted by God, is like a painful execution. It causes pain because it creates chaos, but at the same time, it forces purification and builds up the desire to return to the Father in the attitude of a trusting child, counting, above all, on His grace.

The devil is not equal to God. He is merely a creature. But God permits us to be exposed to his temptations. Fatherly love is not overprotective, not allowing us to face real challenges. Like a good Father, God pushes us out into the real world, where we experience difficulties and, at the same time, learn the value of goodness and the power of the summoned divine grace.

We are not left alone in this. In His death, Jesus voluntarily surrendered Himself to the forces of evil, and all during the Passion, He loved both the Father and us to the very end. By pointing to the supreme infinite love of the Son, dramatically manifested in that death, the Father showed us the way out of the trap. It is as if He said: "Take hold of My Son. His infinite gift is of such value that you can use it, like a token that covers your trespasses." Grasping the power of this love sets us free from sins.

The man who wishes to understand himself thoroughly ... must with his unrest, uncertainty and even his weakness and sinfulness, with his life and death, draw near to Christ.

St. John Paul II

The gift of supreme love flowing from the open Heart of Jesus and embraced by faith heals the weakness of the will and frees it from the confusion that is the direct result and punishment of sin. In this process of healing and release, the natural human sense of justice is respected. Sin is real, and we do not want a cheap grace that downplays evil. We know that a serious reaction is due, and it is precisely that which is shown to us in Jesus' voluntary gift of Himself.

The fact that Jesus takes upon Himself the consequences of sin may be called "redemption" or "satisfaction," but this is not to be understood too literally. Our discernment, disapproving of evil, has been respected, and so the due has been paid — not to the devil or to the offended Father but to our sense of justice. This sense is an echo of our natural, innermost carnal, sensual, and spiritual inclinations, which have their proper ends, and that is why they always react with a dissonance whenever they are distorted.

Evil is thus overcome by the immeasurable power of Jesus' love, to which we have access through faith. The executioner, employed by God, who unwittingly calls for conversion is suddenly beaten off his track by the magnitude of this completely unforeseen love.

Therefore, we should certainly not claim that Jesus assuaged the terrible wrath of the Father. Jesus unveiled and expressed the love of the heavenly Father in the best, clearest way possible, and it is with this that the Father is greatly pleased. We can visualize this by imagining the parents of a doctor who traveled to a distant country and there, while serving the poor, contracted a tropical disease and died. Being informed of this death, his parents will, of course, feel grief, but on hearing of his generosity, they will feel, on a deeper spiritual level, a certain joy. They wanted their son to be a good person, and now they are glad that love has triumphed in his heart, to the very end.

He it was, and He alone, who satisfied the Father's eternal love.

St. John Paul II

The heavenly Father was pleased not with the cruelty of Jesus' death but with the quality of love that animated it from within. St. John Paul II wrote (in Polish) that, in this way, Jesus *fied satis* the eternal love of the Father. The pope did not use the word "satisfied." Grammatically, in Polish, the two expressions seem to mean the same thing, yet with different focuses. When a child kicks a ball that then smashes a neighbor's window and his father pays to replace the window, we say that he has satisfied for the harm suffered. The work of Jesus was not such a legal satisfaction for our sins but, above all, a wonderful gift of the entire Blessed Trinity that allows us to base ourselves on a love that is more powerful than all of our errors, missteps, and sins.

He raised up the daughter of the synagogue official while she was still lying in the house; he raised up the widow's young son after he had been carried beyond the gates of the city; he raised up Lazarus, who had been buried for four days.... Sin is the death of the soul. But sometimes one sins in thought.... The Lord, signifying that he raises up such a soul, raised up that girl, who had not yet been carried out, but was lying dead in the house, as if the sin was hidden. But if you not only consented to the evil delight, but also did the evil deed itself, you have, as it were, carried the dead beyond the gate; you are now outside, you have been carried out, dead. And yet the Lord also raised him up and restored him to his mother, the widow. If you have sinned, repent! The Lord raises you up, too, and will return you to your mother, the Church. The third dead person is Lazarus.... He who sins habitually has been buried and it is well said of him, "He stinks." For he begins to have the worst reputation, like the foulest odor. Such are all who are accustomed to crimes, abandoned in character.... And yet, no less was the power of Christ for raising him up. We know, we have seen, every day we see men live better, after the worst habit has been changed, than they who were reproaching them live.

St. Augustine

XVII. Afterword

I announced in the preface that I would not be describing a wealth of emotional experiences in this book. My aim was more modest. I was concerned with explaining how the emotions function and what their place in the psyche is, and therefore how they are integrated with the spiritual powers. In doing so, I pointed out the influence of grace manifested in the psyche and in the free acts of the person who is maintaining a relationship with God. I then discussed typical disorders that occur that introduce emotional disorder and hinder trust in oneself. The naming and precise identification of the basic components of the psyche required a discourse that is inherently rational, one might say, to the bone.

This means that I primarily described the skeleton and its possible deviations, but of course, we know that a living human being is more than just bones. It is in the whole person, made up of body and soul, and therefore also having emotions, human experiences take place. Feelings bring a lively, pulsating dynamic, color, and flavor, as well as pain. This is primarily felt and experienced, while reflection on the nature of the emotions is always secondary. First there is life, and only then comes thinking about this life, about its nature, its development, or about degeneration that occurs and calls for healing.

Svetlana Alexievich, literary Nobel laureate from Belarus, recounts the memory of a woman serving in the Red Army. In 1945, in Berlin, amid the rubble, dirt, smoke, wounds, mutilations, and omnipresent death, with the smell of blood, the tragedy of war, and the joy of victory, her fellow-in-arms proposed marriage to her. At that moment, she burst out crying and wanted to hit him. This was not how she had imagined this moment. She wanted her future husband to notice her, to give signals, to follow her with his eyes, to appreciate her feminine charms, to court her with tender words, to show gestures of kindness and give her flowers. In the meantime, in the frontline maneuvers, their attention was completely focused on the war, on carrying out orders and defeating the enemy in the hope that, through victory, death would be avoided. Everything was dirty and gray, including their torn-up uniforms. In the terrible fatigue, in fear and in the midst of battle, there was no room for courtship and affection, for the charm that her feminine heart had been waiting for. The proposal had been made suddenly and unexpectedly, and the stages necessary for the awakening of love, which take their time and need to mature, had been skipped over. How can one live and remember this one moment, so important in life, when what touches and thrills the heart is missing? Her sudden outburst of rage induced shame in him. He understood, and tears streamed down his red, tanned cheek and over the fresh scars of war. And she accepted his proposal.

In the feeling of love, there is excitement; there is delight, longing, and desire. There is ardor, attention, the noticing of details and anxious waiting for kind gestures. There is caring concern, and kindness manifested in smiles and pleasant words. But opposite emotions also add their strength to love. Crying, anger, rage, and indignation express the total rejection of that which opposes love. When the stages of contact have been skipped over and the gestures have turned out to be quick, possessive, insensitive to the glimmer of nascent love and to the slow pace of its maturation, a doubt arises as to whether the signals in question are genuine or whether they are hypocritical and inauthentic.

In authentic love, there is also room for sadness and pain, which stems from concern for the other person, from taking on his or her problems, worries, pains, illnesses, wrongs suffered, and even sins. If it has happened that the loved one has hurt someone, he has also and even primarily, hurt himself. "What have you done to yourself?" says the lover to the criminal. She is not only concerned about the wrong that he has done, but also and above all, she is worried that he has fallen into the vortex of sin, and this is what worries her most because she cares about him and she wants him to become a better person.

Emotions sometimes unleash hatred filled with indignation and desire for revenge for the wrong suffered, and this gives courage to stand up for honesty and order. These emotions activate psychic power, but they also need to be controlled, so that hatred does not dissociate human bonds for long. One must therefore learn to distinguish between remembering suffered wrongs and forgiving them. One may go hand in hand with the other. Forgiveness does not require forgetting, but it does require a spiritual insight that reaches further and deeper than remembering, for with the eye of faith, one appeals to the redemptive power of God, and with this received divine love, one reaches to the hidden layer of the other, to his fundamental goodness, which continues even when it has been obscured by actual evil.

In the face of great tragedies, words about feelings prove to be helpless. Traumatic experiences of wars and catastrophes and, what is worse, of inhumane, although sometimes human, but unimaginable wrongs, are sometimes so incomprehensible and surprising that one does not know what to feel and how to express it. Such experiences are covered with silence, but they persist in the depths of the psyche and sometimes come to light only years later, in an encounter with true kindness. They can then be uttered and finally healed with the power of forgiveness and Christian hope.

Fervent, concerned, and at the same time tender, patient, and forgiving love revealed in affectionate contact is an icon depicting the mysterious love of God. Such fully human, emotional language was used by God in expressing His love to us. The history of salvation is a long, patient unveiling of the truth that God loves us. His love, shown first to the Chosen People but actually applying to each one of us, is a long string of given signals. God pursues the beloved with His eyes, with His signals, with His gestures. He whispers in the ear of those who respond to Him with faith and invites them to follow in His steps.

The love of God is merciful; this means that it encompasses His whole interior. God is spirit, without a body, but His love is as if corporeal, as if asking for a body and emotions, so that it may express itself with heartfelt compassion in a human way. The need to manifest this fully human, warm dimension of divine love, which goes further than the love found in the will, is one of the most profound motives for the Incarnation. In Christ, true God and true man, God's love has been fully shown in a human fashion. It is true that God's concern sometimes manifested itself in words of anger and indignation, but ultimately God has been revealed in the flesh and in the humanity of the Infant, and then this love of God was even more profoundly disclosed in the total gift of Jesus Himself, given on the Cross.

The divine signals that follow man are not meant to go unheeded. It is true that we may not notice them or may notice them and simply not care, but God is patient and "timid." He does not want to put us in the foolish position when He has spoken to us and we ignored Him, and that is why He is so careful in His gestures. It is only when a person responds, even modestly, meagerly but genuinely, that God's promptings, evidence of His closeness and invitation, become more frequent. The book of Psalms is a collection of poetry written by people who were sensitive to God and responded to Him. It covers the whole range of human emotion, from awe, gratitude, love, petition, and blessing to anger and indignation. Every mood, necessarily changeable but true at a given moment, finds its expression there. It is no wonder that, for centuries, the Church has used the psalms in her prayer, for there are the words and feelings of God, and the words and feelings of man, who recognizes the pursuing gestures of God and responds to them.

Each one of us has his or her own story of communion with God, and it bears fruit in deeds. The Gospel shows us a Samaritan who recognized the divine call of love, was deeply moved, and trusted God so much so that, in his goodness, divine mercy was revealed. Our gestures too, even the seemingly weakest ones, can be vehicles of God's mercy. So we could describe this adventure of our communion with God in our own personal psalms, full of wonder, hope, goodness, sorrow, and gratitude.

The bond with God that takes place through faith and charity transforms the whole person, with all conscious, courageous, and creative choices and feelings. This is what has been sketched out in this book. Giving this skeleton a vivid, dynamic content is the life story of every one of us.

FURTHER READING

Wojciech Giertych, O.P., *Spark of Faith: Understanding the Power of Reaching Out to God* (Irondale, AL: EWTN Publishing, 2018).

Servais Théodore Pinckaers, O.P., *Passions and Virtue* (Washington D.C.: Catholic University of America Press, 2015).

Servais Théodore Pinckaers, O.P., *The Sources of Christian Ethics* (Washington D.C.: Catholic University of America Press, 1995).

Servais Théodore Pinckaers, O.P., *The Pursuit of Happiness — God's Way: Living the Beatitudes* (Staten Island, NY: Alba House, 1998).

Nicholas E. Lombardo, O.P., *The Logic of Desire: Aquinas on Emotion* (Washington D.C.: Catholic University of America Press, 2011).

Conrad Baars and Anna A. Terruwe, *Psychic Wholeness and Healing: Using All the Powers of the Human Psyche*, 2nd ed. (Staten Island, NY: Alba House, 1981).

Conrad Baars and Anna A. Terruwe, *Healing the Unaffirmed: Recognizing Emotional Deprivation Disorder* (Staten Island, NY: Alba House, 2002).

Jordan Aumann, O.P., and Conrad Baars, *The Unquiet Heart: Reflections on Love and Sexuality* (Staten Island, NY: Alba House, 1991).

Bl. Marie-Eugene of the Child Jesus, *Where the Spirit Breathes* (Staten Island, NY: Alba House, 1998).

CITATIONS

Preface. Zagadka [Riddle], in Cyprian Norwid, *Vade-mecum* (Wrocław: Ossolineum, 2003), 105. All biblical citations are taken from *The Jerusalem Bible* unless otherwise stated.

I. *Ad I Cor.*, chap. 15, l. 2 (924), *Commentary on the Letters of Saint Paul to the Corinthians*, trans. F. R. Larcher, B. Mortensen, and D. Keating (Lander, WY: Aquinas Institute for the Study of Sacred Doctrine, 2012), 349; *Catechism of the Catholic Church*, no. 1773; *The Christian Faith in the Doctrinal Documents of the Catholic Church*, ed. J. Neuner and J. Dupuis (Staten Island, NY: Alba House, 2001), 512.

II. *Summa Theologiae* Ia-IIae, q. 74, art. 3, ad 1 (my translation); *II Ethic*, chap. 6 (1106b36), in *The Complete Works of Aristotle*, vol. 2, ed. J. Barnes (Princeton: Princeton University Press, 1995), 1748; *Passions and Virtue*, trans. B. M. Guevin (Washington, DC: Catholic University of America Press, 2015), 2.

III. *Gaudete et exsultate* (2018), no. 34; Letter 142, in *General Correspondence*, vol. 2, trans. J. Clarke (Washington, D.C.: Institute of Carmelite Studies, 1988), 795.

IV. 1 Cor. 1:9, Revised Standard Version, Catholic Edition; *Story of a Soul*, trans. J. Clarke (Washington, D.C.: Institute of Carmelite Studies, 1975), Manuscript C, 35r, 256; Hom. 21 (CCL 122, 151), Office of Readings, feast of St. Matthew, September, 21.

V. Fr. Pierre-Etienne, Arrangement: Dominican Friars (Kraków, 1998), 206.

VI. Letter 144, in *General Correspondence*, vol. 2, trans. J. Clarke (Washington, D.C.: Institute of Carmelite Studies, 1988), 803–804; *Passions and Virtue*, trans. B. M. Guevin (Washington, D.C.: Catholic University of America Press, 2015), 62.

VII. *Summa Theologiae*, Ia-IIae, q. 68, art. 4 (Blackfriars, 1974, vol. 24, trans. E. D. O'Connor); *Ad II Cor.*, chap. 12, l. 3 (472), *Commentary on the Letters of Saint Paul to the Corinthians*, trans. F. R. Larcher, B. Mortensen, and D. Keating (Lander, WY: Aquinas Institute for the Study of Sacred Doctrine, 2012), 601; PN 51, v. 2, "An Un-Petaled Rose," in *Poems of St. Thérèse of Lisieux*, trans. A. Bancroft (London: HarperCollins, 1996), 163; *Conseils et Souvenirs*, quoted in Marie-Eugène, *I Am a Daughter of the Church* (Chicago: Fides Publishers, 1955), 406.

VIII. *I Polit.*, chap. 5 (1254b4), in *The Complete Works of Aristotle*, vol. 2, ed. J. Barnes (Princeton: Princeton University Press, 1995), 1990; *Summa Theologiae*, Ia-IIae, q. 58, art. 3, ad 2 (Blackfriars, 1969, vol. 23, trans. W. D.

Hughes); *The Idea of a University* (Oxford: Clarendon Press, 1976), 164–165, quoted in I. Ker, *Newman on Vatican II* (Oxford: Oxford University Press, 2014), 115.

IX. *Commentary on the Letter of Saint Paul to the Romans*, chap. 5, l. 6 (454), trans. F. R. Larcher (Lander, WY: Aquinas Institute for the Study of Sacred Doctrine, 2012,); *Summa Theologiae*, IIa-IIae, q. 152, art. 2, ad 2 (Blackfriars, 1968, vol. 43, trans. T. Gilby).

X. Homily for the Inauguration of the Pontificate (October 22, 1978), *Acta Apostolicae Sedis* 70 (1978), 947 (my translation); *Donner sa vie: Dix jours de retraite sur l'Eucharistie* (Paris: Cerf, 2003), 40 (my translation).

XI. Letter 258, in *General Correspondence*, vol. 2, trans. J. Clarke (Washington, D.C.: Institute of Carmelite Studies, 1988), 1153.

XII. *Summa Theologiae*, Ia-IIae, q. 31, art. 7 (Blackfriars, 1975, vol. 20, trans. E. D'Arcy); *Sent. Ethic.*, bk. 6, l. 2, no. 8, 1131, trans. C. I. Litzinger (Notre Dame, IN: Dumb Ox Books, 1993); Ps. 130:1, Jubilee Bible; *Veni Sancte Spiritus*, 7–8 (translated by J. M. Neale).

XIII. *Humanae Vitae* 11–12 (my translation).

XIV. From a collection of proverbs published by Vladimir Dahl in 1862, quoted in Daniel Rancour-Lafferiere, *The Slave Soul of Russia: Moral Masochism and the Cult of Suffering* (New York: New York University Press, 1995), 13; ibid., 64; homily, Victory Square, Warsaw, June 2, 1979.

XV. *The Development of Morality* (Komorów: ANTYK, 2020), 482; *The Sources of Christian Ethics* (Washington, D.C.: Catholic University of America Press, 1995), 466; *Passions et vertu* (Paris: Parole et Silence, 2009), 44 (my translation); *Traité pratique ou le moine*, 12, 1–4 (Paris: Sources chrétiennes 171, 1971), 520–522 (my translation); *Parochial and Plain Sermons*, vol. 5, 314–316, quoted in I. Ker, *Newman on Vatican II* (Oxford: Oxford University Press, 2014), 138.

XVI. *Redemptor Hominis* 10, 9; *In Evangelium Ioannis Tractatus*, 49, 3 (PL 35), in *Tractates on the Gospel of John* 28–54, trans. J. W. Rettig (Washington, D.C.: Catholic University Press, 1993,), 240–241.

XVII. *The Unwomanly Face of War*, quoted from the Polish edition, *Wojna nie ma nic z kobiety*, trans. J. Czech (Wołowiec, 2018), 12–13.

IMAGES

Page 5. Council of Trent in the Basilica of St. Mary Major, by Elia Naurizio (1589–1657)

Page 17. Casa Rosada (Argentina Presidency of the Nation)

Page 28. *Resurrection*, by Szymon Czechowicz

Page 40. Eric Gaba/Sting

Page 72. Stephen Langton

Page 87. Feliks Koneczny, sketch by Velogustlik

ABOUT THE AUTHOR

Fr. Wojciech Giertych is a Polish Dominican, born in 1951 in London. Since 2005 he has been the Theologian of the Papal Household. He is also a consultor in the Dicastery for the Doctrine of the Faith and in the Dicastery for the Causes of Saints. Since 1994, he has been a professor at the Pontifical University of St. Thomas — the Angelicum in Rome. He lives in the Vatican.